HIDE & SEEK
TIGER

Praise for *Eighteen Tides and a Tiger*

"Uniting pace, a symbol of courage and along with that a character from a fairy tale to link old and new, So that a bridge is formed between the heroic, romantic traditions of the past and today's modern world."

—Vijayluxmi Bose

"One of the reasons why such books are important is because they serve as handy introductions to our unique ecosystems and give an insight into the need to maintain environmental balance. Tiger conservation, in particular, has received overwhelming publicity and support. Perhaps, if the same could be extended to other environmental causes, there would be a less foolhardy generation who will treat their environment with the respect it deserves."

—Indian Express

"The entire book is an adventure oozing with thrilling mysteries and intriguing characters. The author's evident message of wildlife conservation was clear, as certain excerpts were read out to the audience, delighting all. Basu skillfully taps into the very essence of life at the Sundarbans, easily visible in her vivid descriptions of the marshy forests."

—Hemalatha Sridhar

HIDE & SEEK TIGER

ANJANA BASU

THE ENERGY AND RESOURCES INSTITUTE

Creating Innovative Solutions for a Sustainable Future

ISBN 978-93-86530-90-5

First published by TERI, 2019

In-text Illustrations: Vijay Nipane

Published by

The Energy and Resources Institute (TERI)

TERI Press	*Tel.*	2468 2100 or 7110 2100
Darbari Seth Block	*Fax*	2468 2144 or 2468 2145
IHC Complex, Lodhi Road		India +91 • Delhi (0) 11
New Delhi – 110 003	*Email*	teripress@teri.res.in
India	*Website*	www.teriin.org

Printed in India

For two R's who have stepped beyond 18, one R who hasn't and a small S who prefers to be an O. Rahul, Rudra, Rohan and Sreeja O

Oro's US Perspective

I read a book about Nitro the tiger. Nitro was blind and lived in a small cage. A stranger came up and put his hand through the feeding hole. Nitro did not live in a zoo. The man had to go to hospital. Nitro's owner went to jail. Nitro went to a place with a bigger cage. It was a zoo. The moral is not to keep tigers or large animals in small cages. Nitro knew his way around his old cage. Once he got a big new cage the zoo keepers led him round with mint and candy till he learnt his way. I first went to the zoo when I was seven – that was when I saw a tiger with my cousins and mom. I don't know if it was Nitro.

The US has the most tigers in private zoos. Sad.

Deet's Poem

The sun filtering through the
trees
down to the dry
leaf covered ground
the little specks of dust
showing a
crystal shine
in the sun

Snap, crunch
a twig, a bush
crumpling leaves

The woods smell
different
the tension so
thick and heavy

What's this the smell of
the hunters' gun
his metal, sweat

It's time to play

The path clear
chirps, creaks, warm sunlight
suddenly
shock

cringes going up and down
my spine
the whispers of
the trees and wind grow

Something's not right

I move slowly
one foot
one paw
in front of the other
who is "it"
in this game
or is it a game

Muscles tensing to
stay, quiet, alert
ready for anything

rustling in the bush

stop
stay
one, two, three

"found you!"

– Aditi Stromayer

Rohan's Foreword
TIGERS, TIGERS, TIGERS...

All these years we have lectured about the importance of the conservation of tigers. Many conservationists came together to lead various movements regarding the saving of this endangered species. In 2014 the tiger population was 2,226 according to statistics. However, India has the capacity to accommodate only 3,000 tigers with 25-35% living outside national parks and reserves, which is why their lives are in danger. Alongside tigers, India's population has already crossed the 1.34 billion mark according to 2017 Census. As a result people are desperately trying to expand their land by cutting down trees and planting farmlands, thereby getting rid of their food and shelter. The tigers having nothing else to eat go to these farms and prey on the cows and goats. If they don't find anything else to eat, they will sometimes attack people; this being one of the main reasons for people being scared and trying to poison or traps tigers.

In May 2019, another tiger count will take place and if it crosses 3000, the forest officials will have to come up with a good idea. Some officials say that countries such as Thailand and Cambodia, which have few or no tigers, will be the right place for the excess Indian tigers. However, I think that it is quite foolish to send those tigers to foreign countries as they will be confused about their surroundings, knowing the fact that they are very territorial in nature. Tigers have their own corridors and thus they wouldn't want any outsiders to enter them. How would the poor tigers feel, entering an unknown and strange habitat? Another factor is the breeding of the species, which they might not want to do in Thailand and Cambodia.

It is quite strange when I start thinking about the sudden growth of tigers in a span of 10 years. I keep on remembering those times when my aunt wrote novels regarding Jim Corbett's ghost and when she gave brief lectures about conservation of tigers on the occasion of her book launches. She had once made us watch a movie related to the poaching of tigers and their highly priced skin trade. She had brought her friend, Rishin Basu Roy, who told us about his experiences in Kanha.

And now when I hear the increase in population of tigers in various news channels, I just can't help but laugh at the irony.

Rudra's Poem

Steel Menagerie

CR's toy,
Crushed dreams of the boy,

Never seen the real
Deal

Will he see the beasts of legend,
Tomorrow when he visits the caged hell,
With rancid smell
Caged in the s★★★
Smelted steel

In simulated reality,
No thrill of the hunt,
No dream of freedom,
No wild to call home but the
Simulation.

Would this be the real
Deal

Going to a fake forest
To see unseen unrest
And a false lost home

Even released,
There is no wild
In these mild
Tigers.

Playing hide-and-go-seek
In the sleek
Steel Menagerie.

Author's Note

The Real Hide and Seek Tiger

"Yellow and black in red country!" shrieked the
headlines. That was the first time that people heard
of the Lalgarh tiger. Lalgarh in the Jhargram region
of Bengal isn't tiger territory at all – it was notorious
for Maoists. Thorny scrublands, hills and sal forests
housed deer and elephant raids from across the border
were common. Then one day a tiger appeared and left
its footprints across the territory. No one had seen it
but word spread like wildfire among the villages and
reached the Forest officials. There was an instant setting
up of camera traps to catch and identify the tiger and a
pale ghostly image appeared in the papers.

Villagers were warned against going out into
the fields at night or taking their cattle to graze too
far from the village. There was an atmosphere of
restlessness and creepiness – everyone in the region
felt that the tiger was stalking them. This was despite
the fact that no one had set eyes on anything except a
pugmark and a photograph.

The worry about clashes between people and tigers
is that tigers eventually always lose out – people dislike
being forced to change their ways simply because India
has grown unused to living with animals these days.

Tigers are frequently killed, especially when they become cattle lifters – though the Government does have a policy of compensation. Where the Lalgarh tiger was concerned it was a matter of who would find it first, the forest department or the villagers. However, in its favour was the fact that the big cat lay low, avoided people and did not seem to be making cattle kills though what it ate was a mystery, since few carcasses were found.

Most people think that a tiger is a tiger is a tiger, but tigers have different subspecies and even in India the Bengal tiger (*panthera tigris tigris*) differs in its habits from state to state. It was supposed that the Lalgarh tiger had crept over the border from Simplipal in Odisha, but no one got a clear look at its stripes to identify it. There was even a suggestion that the cat had come up from the Sunderbans though that was too far away for even a free-ranging tiger to roam. However, the Sunderbans tiger experts were called in, and Sunderbans tactics were used to trap a tiger in territory that was very different from the mysterious marshes of the lands of the eighteen tides. In the Sunderbans, tigers that strayed into villages could be netted. However in Jhargram, villages were spread out, and cornering a tiger was difficult – especially when the forest department lacked resources.

The game of tiger hide and seek was played out through culverts with moments of now you see it, now you don't. The tiger was trapped once but roared its way out of the fishing net – the men holding it over the culvert entrances were terrified and dropped the net. Everyone felt the tiger's eyes in their back but no one could see anything. Elephants ultimately destroyed the camera traps, making the game even harder. There was talk of bringing in sniffer dogs. Drones were sent out in search of the elusive big cat, but the tree cover made it impossible to locate.

Matters were complicated by the local tribal hunting festival that took place at the end of March, the end of the year in Bengal. Anticipating this, one of the forest department members, a woman, begged the village pradhans not to let their villages go hunting at any rate to spare the tiger.

Ultimately, a tiger which did its best to avoid humans was speared and paraded on the shoulders of a triumphant group of young men who clicked selfies – after the villagers had haggled with the Forest Officials over how much money they would get for carrying the dead cat to the Department's truck. An FIR was filed because killing tigers is against the law but so far no one has been arrested.

This story is based on the Lalgarh tiger.

1

The tiger streaked out of the culvert and across the open ground into the bushes. In the darkness, it was just another patch of moonlight and striped shadow, as restless as the shadows thrown by the palm trees overhead. It darted from bush-to-bush and tree-to-tree thankful that none of those tall monkey-like creatures were around. If anyone had looked at the culvert, they would have seen its eyes glowing in the dark as it sniffed the wind before slipping out. The wind was clean and the tiger was thankful that it had found shadows to hide, instead of the cave that smelled of humans; and now with the open forest in front of him, perhaps deer or wild pig could be hunted.

The tree shadows led it to a small stream and as the tiger crossed, it stepped into mud and left a pugmark on the bank – just slippery ground, nothing to bother a big cat. The tiger moved on and soon the shadows were still except for the restless wind.

At dawn, Habu came by with his cows, twisting their tails and cursing. He was half-an-hour late and his father had made him run to get the cows out to graze on time. Cows had been disappearing from time to time, an odd one here, an odd one there, all over the district and word had been spreading. No one was quite sure what was happening – a cow thief perhaps or a wolf. "Perhaps we need a *gaurakshak*," someone had joked, but no one found that funny. Habu had a neem twig between his teeth, and between chewing that and twisting tails, he didn't notice anything on the path until the cows suddenly grunted and refused to move another step. "Arré what's wrong!" Habu yelled with a mouthful of twig twisting the tail of the cow nearest to him extra hard. The cow flinched but refused to move and the others were equally obstinate. One turned and threatened Habu with its stubby horns, while the others began to moo and tried to break away. Something was obviously wrong; Habu went around the cows grumbling at them as he did so. A little away was the small stream that they crossed every morning on their way to the grazing grounds.

There were birds twittering in the trees and the black and orange stripes of the morning sun. Habu looked around and saw nothing unusual. It was just another morning in the forest. "Idiot cows," he muttered and threw his neem twig away in frustration. It landed beside the stream and it was then that Habu saw the pugmark. He had never seen a tiger's paw print before in his 10 years of living in Lalgarh, but it was quite obvious that it belonged to a tiger – what else could it be. Once he got over the shock, he bolted, taking the cows that were only too happy to run with him.

Luckily for Habu and the cows nothing came out of the trees after them and finally he got to his courtyard all out of breath. "Foolish boy!" shouted his father. "What have you done now?"

"*Ba…ba..bbagh!* Baba, tiger!" panted Habu. Habu's mother was bringing water from the tube well. She jerked to a stop, spilling the water. "Tiger? *Orre baba!*"

"A tiger in Lalgarh?" his father snorted. "Have you woken up yet? God knows you slept long enough!"

Habu replied indignantly, "I'll show you if you don't believe me." And then turned, leaving the milling cows behind him.

"Wait, mad boy!" said his father uneasily, wondering whether his son had actually seen something. "If it's a tiger, we can't go empty handed. We need a gun!" The moment the word was out of his mouth, Habu's father looked around in alarm. Though Lalgarh was named after the ruined Muslim fortress in the jungle as it was red, at one point, Lalgarh had bristled with guns because of the Maobadis who prowled the jungles and occasionally popped into the villages to demand food or medicine or some other kind of help. It had been a while that the Maoists had faded back into the jungles from where they had originally come, the word gun was a strict no-no and police still sprang surprise checks in case there were any guns hidden in the cowsheds and haystacks.

Habu stamped his foot. "Let's go see," he said.

The village priest came across the fields carrying a brass pot in one hand and untwining his sacred thread from his ear with the other. Ducking the cows, Habu's mother made a dash for his feet. "Pandit *Moshai, bachao*, save us!"

"What's happened?" asked the priest startled. He had finished his toilet business in the fields and was looking forward to breakfast – well no, not breakfast, first the morning puja for the village women, but…

"Tiger!" cried Habu's mother. "My son's seen a tiger!"

Her high-pitched voice set heads turning. Other villagers came running to see what the excitement was all about.

One of them had a sickle on his shoulder and was obviously on his way to the fields. "*Orree baba, baagh!*" cried the priest, just managing to hold onto his brass pot.

"There's a weapon," said Habu's father pointing at the sickle. It was a babble of voices causing utter confusion and the cows did not help. Habu twisted their tails again in sheer frustration. "I didn't see a tiger!" he shouted.

The babble stopped and everyone looked at him. "What rubbish! What is this boy saying?" the priest asked.

Habu's father stepped forward, hand raised to slap him. "Come and see," said Habu. "I'll show you. And bring that sickle."

"You can't kill a tiger," said the priest. "The officials will come down on us."

"Not if it attacks us first," said the man with the sickle, his eyes gleaming at the prospect of fighting a tiger early in the morning.

"It's better to talk to the Pradhan first," the priest suggested. "He'll know what to do." The rest of them nodded and one of them went to fetch the Pradhan from his hut. Habu was shifting from foot to foot in irritation. With all this talk he thought, something was bound to happen to the paw print he had seen – some idiot would cycle over it or cattle would tread over it once the scent was gone. Grown-ups, however, could not be hurried – all he would get for his pains would be a slap from his father and rice water for lunch.

Mohan Das, the Pradhan, was pulled out of his newspaper and told the story – as well as the villagers could tell it. "Who saw this?" Mohan Das asked and Habu was finally pushed to the front by his father. He explained what had happened in the morning. The Pradhan nodded and eyed the man with the sickle. "That sickle is only for use in the fields, Dinen. Let the forest department deal with the tiger – if there is a tiger."

"Then what do we do?" Dinen demanded, looking disappointed. "Pull out the festival bows and arrows?" The Pradhan was about to say something when there was the sound of a cycle bell and a young man rode up to the Pradhan's hut on his bicycle. "What's this?" he asked. "A meeting, and that too so early in the morning?"

"You have a smart phone, don't you Master Moshai?" Mohan Das asked. "Then go with them and see what Habu is talking about. He says he's seen a tiger." The young man, who was the school teacher, raised an eyebrow. But he obediently turned his cycle and they all went off together, leaving the Pradhan to return to the morning news and Habu's mother to deal with the cows.

The procession was a noisy one and Habu was certain that they would scare away everything within a kilometre's radius. He wanted to see a tiger because Lalgarh had never seen or heard of one and he had grown up while more dangerous things were happening in the jungles.

Master Moshai rode in front on them and Habu shouted to him to slow down. "You don't know where we're going!"

"Where are we going?" the school teacher asked sceptically. "I've never seen a tiger in these forests!"

Habu explained about the grazing meadow and the small stream, and Master Moshai pedalling furiously whisked out of sight, occasionally tinkling the cycle bell. "Everyone knows everything," Habu's father grumbled. "Serves him right if the tiger gets him!"

With the sickle ready, the rest of the group finally caught up with Master Moshai's bicycle. He had stopped in a glade behind a small hillock. "The stream is down there," he said pointing. "I thought we should go together. There's a culvert nearby and anything could be hiding there." Closely grouped together they walked over the hillock to the stream. It was a normal morning, the birds were chirping, a squirrel on the ground cocked his head at them and then swam smoothly up the nearest tree trunk.

Habu couldn't bear it any longer — he ran up to the bank of the stream. The paw print was still there and nothing had trodden over it. "It's here!" he called.

The group of men clustered around it. "*Baagh na nekreybaagh?*" Dinen demanded. "Must be a wolf, not a tiger."

Habu's father scratched his head, "Could be a tiger. Doesn't look like a wolf or a jackal. We'll have to tell the forest department. Master Moshai, what do you think?"

"I've never heard of a tiger in these parts," Master Moshi said. "But it looks like a tiger's paw print." He fumbled on the side of his kurta and pulled out his phone. It was a new one he had bought on his trip to Raniganj and everyone in the village had been eyeing it surreptitiously. Carefully focusing, he bent down and clicked the pugmark. "I'll google it just to make sure," he added.

His class was in awe of him because their teacher was so technologically advanced. "He does all this Google shoogle stuff so easily!" they marvelled. This was apart from the fact that he was a relaxed kind of teacher who had never been known to cane anyone.

"It's a tiger's paw print all right," the Master Moshi announced. "We'll have to inform the forest department. Now we'd better get back and tell Mohan Babu." And even as he spoke, he continued to fiddle with his phone.

By the time they got back to the Pradhan's hut, Master Moshai's phone had been ringing continuously. Habu caught the snatches of conversation, "Haanh, *baagh*....never been one in Lalgarh...pugmark you saw it..." Master Moshai spoke in English from time to time so not all of it made sense but he was obviously spreading the news about the tiger to everyone he knew.

"You've told everyone," said the Pradhan after the phone had rung a few times in his presence, "but have you informed the forest department?"

"Eh...no, Pradhan Moshai," said Master Moshai. "I thought you should do that...village Pradhan after all..."

The Pradhan glared at him. "It's a good thing you do leave some things to me," he said. "After those Maoist friends of yours created all that chaos..."

The Master Moshai flinched at that and the men exchanged glances behind him. No one had been able to avoid the Maoists, and some of them were Master Moshai's classmates from the town. It was because of them that he had come to Lalgarh and started teaching in the village school. The bigger cities refused to give him a job. It was also why he had bought that smart phone so recently – the police had finally returned his confiscated sim card on the Pradhan's entreaties.

The Maoists had been tigers of a sort, lurking in the forests, Habu thought, and occasionally walking into the village to demand food or taking a goat when they felt like it. No one strayed far from the village in the evenings if they could help it – except over the last six years when things had changed and the forests were calm again. A few people had thought the Maoists were taking the missing cattle but no one wanted to voice it – now, however, the disappearances were beginning to make sense.

Ignoring the Master Moshai's pale face, the Pradhan brought out his own phone and flipped through his contacts. His was a battered old Nokia. With a grunt, he dialled a number. Then he turned to Master Moshi and said, "Now send that photograph you took to the Divisional Forest Officer. He wants to see it." And with that, word of the unexpected tiger began to spread over Bengal.

2

Rohan was sitting in his class trying to make sense of physics when the phone in his pocket jumped. It was banned in class so he continued looking at the teacher and scribbling notes. Not that he was expecting anything important – it was either his mother or an ad. After class he went out into the corridor and was shoving his way to the next lesson when the phone in his pocket jerked again and he remembered that he had not checked it. There was a WhatsApp message from an unknown number. Rohan was wary about unknown numbers; they came out of the datasphere and flooded his phone with alarming messages. He cautiously clicked it open and saw a photograph of a tiger's pugmark taken at fairly close range. He stared at the photo and swam his fingers over the screen to enlarge it – only to push the phone back into his pocket as the bell rang for the next class. However, the pugmark kept nagging at him and earned him a reprimand from Ms D'Silva, who taught geography. "Considering you've been to the Sunderbans," she said, "you should be more informed about the soil conditions of the Ganges Delta."

When he had time to look at his phone again, a WhatsApp message from the Khan Sahib with the same pugmark had joined the first one. The Khan Sahib's photograph had a terse caption 'Clicked at Lalgarh'. He frowned at the word 'Lalgarh' – the only tigers he knew about in Bengal were the ones in the Sunderbans, where he had interned at Sajnekhali and Jharkhali over the summer, not to mention losing himself and spending a night in a boat with a strange girl. The other unknown number was part of a Forestry WhatsApp Group and had no profile picture either, which was irritating, so it could not be Rishin Babu.

That evening he skyped the Khan Sahib.

"Ah, so you got my WhatsApp," the Khan Sahib

said cheerfully. Another face peered into the screen from behind him and Rohan saw that the Major was there too. "What do you want me to do about it?" Rohan asked.

"There has never been a tiger in that area before. I gather that the forest department is sending people with tranquilliser guns to trap it." For a moment, the Khan Sahib was quiet.

"Tell the boy what you want him to do," the Major said.

"Well ask Rishin what he thinks. Have you heard from Rishin?"

"No," Rohan answered, "but someone else WhatsApped the pugmark to me. I don't know the number though." Very carefully, trying not to disconnect, he read the contact information out to the Major and the Khan Sahib. They looked at each other doubtfully and shook their heads. "Is Lalgarh close to you?" the Major asked.

Rohan looked doubtful. "Somewhere in the 24 Parganas, I suppose. "The conversation was not very satisfactory because the Major and the Khan

Sahib were both a little worried by the sudden appearance of a tiger in a place where no tigers had been seen before. It could possibly have wandered down from Similipal in Odisha where no one was keeping count of the tigers. Rohan was in favour of Nepal – after all, the Champawat maneater had come from there – and tigers were in the habit of roaming vast stretches in search of prey or even a mate. The uncles looked at each other doubtfully on a screen that was getting increasingly blurry. "Do some research," they said before the line cut off. "And try and talk to Rishin."

Research was easy – he pulled out the topographical maps of West Bengal and pored over them with such enthusiasm that he didn't miss a single question on the soil of West Bengal in geography class. Ms D'Silva looked suitably impressed and gave him an 'A' for the unit test. Lalgarh he discovered was in West Midnapore and had a patch of forest. More to the point, it and the Malkhedi Forest were in Jhargram where an uncle of his had a garden house in which he was trying to grow avocados. A weekend in Jhargram sounded like a good idea, Rohan thought.

Similipal, he knew, had dropped off the tiger tourism map after outbreaks of malignant malaria. What was odd was that no one had reported finding dead cows anywhere – if it had been in the Kumaon, everyone would have been talking about it. Armed with his 'A' in geography, Rohan went to his mother. Do you think Bablu Mama would let me go to his *baganbari* next weekend?" It was a long weekend, and perhaps the tiger would still be prowling around then.

His mother looked at him. "What is this? Another project of yours?" He nodded, his fingers crossed behind his back. Projects got extra grades and padded the CV that he knew his ambitious mother was getting ready for his undergraduate studies. "I'll talk to Bablu Mama," she said slowly. "If he has a caretaker there, it shouldn't be a problem. But you can't go there on your own."

Getting hold of Rishin Babu was not so easy – his line was either engaged or switched off. The papers were full of rumours that once the Lalgargh tiger was trapped, they would try to shift it to Jharkhali, where Sunderbans tigers in distress were kept. Rohan knew that Rishin Babu would not be in favour of the move. Sunderbans tigers were altogether another breed – they swam, they climbed trees, ate humans from time to time – even Jim Corbett, he was sure, would have been at a loss. He wouldn't have believed it himself if he hadn't seen those mysterious marshy forests with his own eyes.

And then there was the matter of the unknown number which had first sent him the pugmark, even though it did belong to Rishin Babu's group.

His friend Manjul would have ordered him to call the sender immediately and put an end to the mystery – he sighed wishing he could get the uncles to send her down from Nainital and knowing that it would not be possible. While Manjul was planning to join the forest department once she finished school, her world was currently filled with studies, looking after her father's cows and helping her mother around their hut. For want of anything better to do, he forwarded the pugmark to her.

Five minutes later, his phone rang. "What?" Manjul's voice demanded from the other end. "You think I haven't seen a tiger's footprint before?"

"Not this one," he answered. "This is from a place called Lalgarh."

"Red Fort? Dilli?" she laughed. "You're pulling my leg."

"No!" he protested. "This is in Bengal and it isn't a Sunderbans tiger either. The Khan Sahib and the Major asked me to do some research on it."

She sighed, "I wish they could find some research for me."

"No *guldars* in the area?" Rohan wanted to know, asking about the leopards that were far more common than tigers around Manjul's village.

"I think *he* told the *guldars* to stay away from the village," she said, referring to the man they had met over their holidays, the one she unceremoniously called a *bhoot* and who they were both sure had once been Jim Corbett and now returned to look after the jungles he loved.

"Have you seen him?" Rohan asked eagerly.

"No," Manjul answered sadly. "You know he only comes if there's some sort of *lafra*. Bye, I have to help Ma milk the cows now."

"She can help of course," the Khan Sahib said when Rohan suggested it. "There's lots of research to be done on tiger corridors in the area. But if you mean can she go down to Bengal, I am not sure unless the Additional Divisional Forest Officer in the area is agreeable. Her name's Purabi."

The fact that there was a lady Forest Officer startled Rohan. But then, he was finding a lot of things about the Lalgarh tiger very surprising indeed.

He got to Rishin Babu first – or rather Rishin Babu called him back. "Planning another internship?"

"No…meaning not just yet…. I wanted to ask you about the Lalgarh tiger."

Rishin Babu sighed heavily on the other end of the line. "So does everyone. And the problem is, no one has seen it yet. They're setting camera traps in Lalgarh to see whether that helps. In the meantime the adivasis in the areas will be celebrating their spring hunting festival and things are going to get out of control if that happens. I hope the Midnapore Forestry Division knows that."

It was beginning, Rohan thought, to sound like something out of a film. Forests, Adivasis out on a hunt and a woman Forest Officer. That evening he prowled on the terrace looking up at the sky. It was dusty at the edges as if the darkness was faded there and above his head the moon was a yellow torchlight bulb, not quite full. The dusty sky began to grow and nibble at the bowl of the moon and Rohan realised that a storm was coming. The palm trees realised it too and began to toss restlessly, their fronds clawing at the sky. A flash blinded him followed by the growl of thunder. He thought of a tiger prowling under that stormy sky and a dry riverbed with rocks behind which a tiger could crouch — a riverbed that would run wild with water during the monsoons — and while he imagined the river he wondered whether the man who had once been Jim Corbett was there with the tiger. Lalgarh was very far from Kumaon.

A shout from his mother sent Rohan scuttling indoors as the first heavy drops of warm rain began to hit the ground.

3

The trouble with a tiger, where there never had been one before, is that everyone starts seeing tigers. At Binpur the conversation over the chai cups was all about where the tiger could have come from and where it would strike next. Someone remembered the leopard that had struck terror into Dheria twenty years ago. "It came creeping out of nowhere and would snatch the goats or even a stray dog if it could find one." The old man sipped the steaming tea - it was boiling hot but his eyes didn't water. "And after all these years a tiger has come to take his place in Jangalmahal."

Within a day there was a jeep with a trailer that came and parked at the thana. The boys of Binpur crowded around peering through the windows of the trailer. "There's a bed in it!" one of boys cried out excitedly. With the forest department officials came a host of media people, some with microphones and film crews and a few with notebooks. The microphone people made a great deal of the old man and his leopard story. A few reporters trekked through the forest to photograph the pugmark all over again, surrounded by a few surprised cows.

The tiger saw the men go past it but kept quiet and still in the shadow of the leaves. It had found an old banyan tree with a hollow at its base shielded by the great gnarled roots. It crept in there, while the squirrels chittered a warning and the birds flew up into the sky. If there had been anyone around, they would have suspected that something was wrong, but the cow pastures were at some distance from the place the tiger had chosen and though there was a watering place, high noon was no time for people to draw water. Hidden by the sunlight and shadow that matched its stripes, the tiger slept.

Late at night it awoke, sniffed the air and crept out of its shelter. A deer by the watering hole started and leapt away. The tiger thought briefly about dinner but the water was more important. It lapped thirstily and then sniffed the air again.

Following the scent of a wild pig, the tiger brushed through the low hanging branches. For a moment, it thought it smelled a trace of something else but the matter of the pig was more important and the tiger moved on. There was a slight flash as it moved and a noise and though it cocked its ears, nothing else happened and it increased its speed as the wind told that the pig was coming in the tiger's direction. Its hunting was quick and clean – the pig just had time for one little squeak.

The tiger dragged it into the bushes and ate most of it before moving on. By the time the sky started to pale and people were stirring in the villages, it was gone like the shadow beast that it was.

Later in the morning, the forest officials tumbled out of their jeeps to the camera trap and found a pale image of a tiger on the film. They slapped each other on the back and drove down to Binpur to brief the villagers and the press. For the people of the area, it was more nervous excitement than they had seen in their peaceful part of Bengal since the Maoists gave up their weapons, and this was excitement of a different kind. "What do you want us to do?" the pradhans asked.

"Don't go far from the village, especially at night. Try to move in groups, not on your own." said the Divisional Forest Officer. "We plan to trap the tiger and release it in another forest. Until then, please be careful – two of our men will be stationed here in the trailer van. Pradhans please inform your villages."

The pale picture of the tiger made it to the papers across the country and flashed on quite a few WhatsApp messages. In Habu's village, Mohan Pradhan put a curfew on the cow-grazing till 8 am. In addition, the boys were to go in groups of three, armed with sticks. As to the fields and toilets, he said they would have to manage behind the huts, or groups of people with lights would have to escort people who wanted to go to the fields – and here he frowned at the village pundit. Master Moshai was told very firmly not to go cycling after sundown.

In the beginning, it was exciting – Habu didn't have to get up before dawn and he and three of his friends bullied the cattle out in the full sunshine morning and spent the rest of the day chattering about tigers and this and that. A pair of men with rifles came to talk to them. The moment they realized that they were juniors, the boys trailed the two forest officials and hitched a ride on the trailer as it bumped into the forest. The men found a suitable clearing close to one of the streams that crisscrossed the forest like silver snakes and parked the trailer there. For a while, the men sat on the grass surrounded by the boys testing their tranquilliser guns and showing off a little as they pointed them at the fruit hanging from nearby trees — though they refused to let the boys handle the guns.

"What are you going to eat?" one of the boys asked. "Should we bring you some food?"

The men shook their heads and said they had brought food with them. Even then, the boys hung around, hoping for a dinner invitation but then the light started falling and the men were getting restless and slapping at the insects that swarmed as evening fell. "You'd better run home," they told the boys. "Any darker and the tiger will come out."

"What about you?" the boys asked.

"We'll lock ourselves into the trailer," the men told them. "No tiger can get in. In any case, tigers don't usually attack cars, you know."

Rather disappointed, the boys took their sticks and ran off into the forest towards their homes and the men got into their trailer and prepared to enjoy a comfortable evening and night.

When the boys returned full of enthusiasm the next morning, the clearing was empty. "What happened?" one of them asked. "Have they gone somewhere?" Another boy went up to the trailer and peered through the window. "They're sleeping," he said and banged cheerfully on the window. But the men inside did not move. They lay huddled in their bedrolls. The boys banged some more and one of them found a stone and threw it at the window. It clunked fairly loudly but the men still did not respond. Finally it began to dawn on them that something was wrong. A few of them went running back to the village to get their fathers. In the meantime, two of them tried the trailer door, but that was latched.

The men came, looked inside, banged on the windows and door and then finally stared at each other in amazement. "They seem to be dead."

"Could it be the tiger?" someone asked fearfully. However, there were no tracks to be seen anywhere around and in any case how could a tiger have got into a locked trailer. Finally, the Pradhan phoned the forest department. Then they squatted grimly around the trailer and waited until the police and forest officials arrived and forced open the trailer door. Inside, the air-conditioning was on full blast and the two men wrapped in covers lay there, looking peacefully asleep.

Binpur and Dheria village went wild with speculation about ghost tigers. It had shape shifted, slipped through the keyhole and suffocated the two men. The women gave little shrieks at that and promised flowers to the nearest temple.

"Carbon monoxide poisoning," the Master Moshai explained in the evening classes that they now had. "They had the air-conditioning on all night with the trailer windows up. They suffocated."

The children had never heard of anything like that before, so air-conditioner poisoning conversations began creeping into all their tiger conversations.

"What else would a Maoist say?" some of the villagers grumbled over their chillums and cigarettes in the evening. "It is quite obviously the work of evil spirits." They all knew that there was a *shankhchunni* who haunted the nearby pond with her bone-white bangles and her cackling laugh – they had never seen her but someone knew someone whose aunts had met the vengeful female ghost. Some of the village shamans suggested witchcraft and were making plans for bonfires at night to ward off evil spirits. "What kind of tiger is this that we can't even hear its roars and growls?" they demanded. The woods were full of stories of weretigers who could not be found because they turned into human beings during the day. The hunting festival was coming up – the arrows would have to be sharpened and struck against magnets to make them effective against spirit tigers. Though the guns had disappeared, there were bows and arrows in plenty.

"The Dilli forest officers are laughing at you," Manjul told Rohan when she next called, sounding very pleased with herself. "They think your officials don't know anything at all!"

"That's so uncool," Rohan cried indignantly. "The guys are dead."

"Yes, it sounds like something you city people might do. Don't forest officers know you get *machhars* in the forest and then to go and kill themselves over machhars? One ghost image of a tiger, and two people dead already. The Khan Sahib wants to go down to Lalgarh as soon as possible. I can't go though," she added regretfully, "I have exams coming up."

The media, not finding the tiger, speculated on foul play for a while and then abandoned the theory.

4

The tiger had passed the trailer late at night. It smelt of people and bad air. It studied the trailer from the cover of the trees and when there was no movement from it, it slunk through the shadows past it and moved on to the next clump of jungle. It could smell elephant; those huge grey rock-like beasts were on the move and coming in his direction. Though it had no fight with the elephants, the tiger did not feel up to a confrontation – at least not until it had some meat in its stomach. Softly, it went pad…pad…pad back to the tree without even stirring a leaf.

When the breeze was clear of elephant's smell, he crept out again and spent some time wondering which direction to take. It wove its way through the jungle following the course of another streamlet to a culvert, careful this time not to step into the mud. There it took shelter for the night.

In the morning, the wind brought the scent of people to its nostrils. Peering out of the darkness of the culvert, it saw two men moving around. They were workers who had come to check the area surrounding the culvert to ensure that the overpass road was in no danger of collapsing. One of them was actually tapping the bank close to the culvert when the other one shouted. The tiger flashed past them like a streak of orange flame sending them jumping for safety. It was so close that its claws actually tore a piece of fabric from one man's shirt. For a while, it ran through the jungle and then, panting, stopped to take shelter. However, the incident had made him angry.

That night, on the move again, it heard the sound of a bird call and stopped in its tracks to listen. If it were a night bird, it would have sensed the tiger and started shrieking out warnings. This bird call was steady, a ting…ting noise. Slowly he moved forward; there was a clearing ahead and a path crossing the clearing.

A shadow was moving down the path with the light behind it. The tiger moved forward – it could see something moving in a strange wobbly manner. One of those creatures – the tiger could smell it. Rage shook it in a wave and its muscles began to gather for a leap that would break the creature's neck. Except that something stood between the tiger and its prey on the road. A shape that looked human but had no smell. It stood in front of the tiger and blocked the wind and the tiger could smell nothing , though it could see the person on the road tinkling like a bird as it went by.

The shape in front of it made the tiger move back. "That way", it seemed to tell the tiger. "Go that way." There had been other no-smell creatures in the forest. They came gibbering out of trees, sometimes like those stupid monkey things, or rose like wisps of smoke from deserted ponds and blocked the tiger's eyes. However, not one of those had communicated in any way that the tiger could understand. This one was directing the big cat to move towards a forked jungle path and the tiger had turned and gone in that direction. As it padded through the undergrowth, it could hear the tinkling growing fainter in the distance.

ohan's Bablu Mama had called to say that he was welcome to the Jhargram bungalow and the caretaker and his wife were willing to look after him for as long as he wanted to stay there.

His mother said firmly, "He's going over the weekend and that's it." Rohan wondered whether that was really it.

There was a bus to Jhargram or if Rohan wanted, he could take the train and the caretaker would come to pick him from the station. Rohan's mother was in favour of the train but Rohan felt that the bus would be more exciting, even though it was a smooth air-conditioned one and not a bumpy overflowing with passengers and goats kind of bus. He would get an extra evening in Jhargram and perhaps could drive back with the uncles. "Three days," his mother warned him as she stood over him supervising his packing. "And take your maths book along. There'll be nothing to do in the evening, so you can finish your practice sums."

When she wasn't looking, he made a face but he knew there was no point arguing. His father was on one of his business trips again but even if he were there, he would have never interfered with Rohan's mother's diktats on homework. There wasn't much packing to be done, just an odd assortment of drab T-shirts, some shorts, and a pair of trousers in case it was thorny jungle and his legs needed protection. Chips and biscuits were more important – he wasn't too sure how the caretaker's wife's cooking would turn out.

The Khan Sahib and the Major had messaged to say that they would go directly to Jhagram after flying to Kolkata and meeting Rohan's mother. If necessary, they would find rooms at the forest department's bungalow or a Circuit House.

Rohan had told his mother that they were joining him but hastily added that they would not ask Bablu Mama for hospitality.

After the trailer disaster, no one had seen the tiger at all. The forest department had announced that it would send a couple of drones to scan the forests in case they spotted anything. Rohan knew that Corbett National Park had invested in a few in case they helped track poachers, but the drones were still lying in some godown because they hadn't worked out how to operate them effectively in thick forest cover.

In the afternoon, his mother escorted him to Esplanade and put him on the bus, double-checking that Rohan had his phone and the charger. He found himself a window seat and settled down. From the seats behind him, he could hear people discussing the tiger.

"You don't know what I heard though," one voice said.

"What?" asked the other, a high pitched, more nervous voice.

"On ABP Ananda this morning, it said that the tiger had attacked someone in Malda. It came out of the bushes and clawed his face."

"Is he alive?" the other voice asked with hushed horror in its tones.

"Oh yes, it ran away after that."

The women next to Rohan was firmly plugged into her phone and obviously not interested in eavesdropping on conversations. The men behind were convinced that the man was very lucky.

To have been attacked by the most feared paws in the jungle and escaped with a scratched cheek – the people in the Sunderbans were always being killed by tigers! From there, it was all about maneaters and one brief mention of Corbett and the Kumaon.

It was odd the way the tiger suddenly came out of nowhere and disappeared again, leaving no tracks or even kills to show where it had been. As he thought, Rohan gazed out of the window and watched the city traffic give way to trucks and trailers loaded with hay. The bus had taken NH16 towards Jhargram and the roads were widening. Next to him the woman continued to WhatsApp.

He watched signs for guesthouses and petrol pumps flash by. After a while he pulled out the sandwiches he had with him and began munching them; he could hear snores from behind.

The bus stopped at a dhaba and people got off, stretched their legs and went to freshen up. Rohan's phone rang. It was his mother to find out how far he had got and whether he had eaten. She also told him the Khan Sahib and the Major had flown in from Nanital and would leave for Jhargram the next day. Rohan clutched his phone and backpack and looked at the jostling crowd. There were pakoras being fried and cups of hot tea on offer. He was tempted by the smell of pakoras but hesitated, wondering whether he should. Around him, he could hear a buzz of 'tiger'. Some people were wondering what would happen if the bus got in late because they had to go further into the interior from the bus station.

Others shrugged, "No one has seen or heard of the tiger after those two idiots gassed themselves. It may be dead too." Rohan waited to hear the tiger attack story again – but perhaps these people at the dhaba hadn't been watching the news, or perhaps it was one of those fake news that people were only too eager to spread, no matter what the subject. His mobile data was off for once—he thought of turning it on but then decided against it – his parents were always complaining about his bills.

Rohan paid a visit to the stinky toilet behind the dhaba, wished he hadn't and came back to the bus feeling vaguely sick. That was the problem with highways and bus rides, though train toilets weren't any better. He washed his hands at a basin and made his way back to the bus. The light was beginning to fall and the shadows on the highway were longer. Cattle meandered down the side tracks being whacked by their cowherds to make them hurry, their hooves churning up the dust. It caught the sunset light and glimmered golden as the cattle disappeared into the shadows.

The landscape along the highway was dotted with trees and scrub interrupted by streams and irrigation ditches. There was a tea stall with a cluster of men and handwritten signs for country liquor shops that were obviously illegal. There were bursts of loud Hindi music from a megaphone set beside a striped pandal festooned with balloons — either a wedding or one of those pujas that were always being celebrated. Rohan's geography had taught him that the people in the region were Santhals who were hunter-gatherers or at least had been hunter-gatherers before they settled down to agriculture. They had their own kinds of worship centring on a male supreme being and traditions of ghosts and spirits. But then, Rohan thought, ghosts and spirits always stalked jungles and, as always, his thoughts went to the forests of Kumaon and the ghost who walked there.

At one point, the bus swerved wildly and the passengers began to shout at the driver. "Has he gone to sleep or what?" The conductor pointed to a tree blocking the way and then turned on the lights in the bus. The bus continued again. The road gradually became narrower and more winding with trees closing in on either side though there was space enough for two buses to pass. Through the darkness, the eyes of a dog dazzled briefly. There must be a village nearby Rohan thought, otherwise where would a dog come from? And the fact that there was a dog meant that there was no tiger nearby. Unless of course the wind was in the wrong direction – there was always a possibility.

Rohan glanced at his watch – the bus was running late. They had probably stopped at the dhaba longer than expected. People had straggled back after their pakoras and tea, quite forgetting that it would be dark soon. Rohan's mother had invited the Khan Sahib and the Major to dinner at the club and promised to call him from there. She would be annoyed to hear that the bus was running late. Considering all the tigers he had faced, Rohan thought that was silly – the bus's headlights dazzled in something else's eyes as it went past. There was a solitary bulb glowing on the porch of a thatched hut and the signboard of a sweet shop. The woman next to him seemed to be fast asleep, still plugged into her phone.

Rohan's own phone rang. The Khan Sahib was on the other side. "We're having a very nice evening with your mother," he said. Rohan could hear the buzz of conversation in the background and realised that his mother was listening in. "Where are you now?"

"Still on the bus."

"Hmm, perhaps we should ask your uncle to tell his caretaker that. I'll tell your mother and call you back." The Khan Sahib hung up.

There were more huts and shops now, and cycle rickshaws went past them tooting their rubber horns. They were passing through a small town. Rohan saw a sign that read Katapahar. Cut mountain or thorny mountain, he wondered because 'cut mountain' seemed strange as a name. People began shuffling. One or two got up, stretched, and pulled down bags from the overhead racks. His phone rang again. "The caretaker knows the bus is late," the Khan Sahib told Rohan. "He's waiting."

"I think we've almost reached," Rohan told him.

"Khan Uncle, have you heard of that tiger attacking anyone?" The bus was turning into a wide area with high overhead arc lights blazing in the darkness. There were porters running and reaching up to the passenger windows. When it finally stopped, there was a crowd at the door. In all the confusion, the phone got disconnected before he could hear the response from the other side. Rohan squeezed his way through and looked around wondering how he would recognise Bablu Mama's caretaker. Then a white placard caught his eye – it had his name on it scrawled in Bengali.

He made his way towards the placard elbowing past the porters and crowd. A grey-haired man was holding it up with a resigned expression on his face. When he saw Rohan, the expression changed. "Are you Sen Babu's nephew?"

"Yes," Rohan said. "Have you been waiting for a long time?"

"That isn't important. Now come, let's get going. It's late." He led Rohan outside the bus terminus area to where a jeep was waiting. "This is Sen Babu's. He uses it to travel around when he is here." Rohan threw his backpack into the rear of the jeep and climbed into the front.

"Let me tell my mother I've reached," he said.

"Yes, do that. She will be worried. I just spoke to her half-an-hour ago." The caretaker started the engine as he spoke and the jeep wheezed and coughed before the engine came to life. Rohan wondered when it had been last used. With a lurch it began to roll and finally picked up speed and moved through the crowded streets. Once it was in motion, Rohan called his mother and reassured her that he had reached and was on his way to his uncle's bungalow. "Good," said his mother. "Oh, the Khan Sahib asked me to tell you that no one was attacked by any tiger. Thank goodness," she muttered under her breath.

Rohan sat back and watched the streets give way to darkness. "What have you come for?" the caretaker asked curiously. "There's no excitement in Jhargram for city children."

"To see the tiger," Rohan said promptly, thinking it was best to be open about it.

"Baagh? Very few people have seen the baagh. I don't think it's here anymore." The jeep turned onto one of those roads that wound through the trees in utter darkness except for the glare of the headlights. "Now if you wanted to see elephants... those come down from the hills quite often."

Elephants and a tiger – they did co-exist in the jungle and national parks and sometimes they had a warning system, though whether a solitary tiger out of its own terrain would be comfortable facing an elephant herd was doubtful. Still, it would be nice to see elephants. The road was narrow and curving and utterly dark. Bablu Mama's caretaker was not a very smooth driver – he took the turns sharply with a squeal of brakes as if he was on a motorbike and speeded on the straight bits. Rohan wondered whether he had ever driven a Kolkata taxi in his past life and grabbed at the side of the jeep on some of the turns. "What's your name?" he asked, hoping to slow things down.

"Ganesh Mahato," the caretaker answered cheerfully. "I'm driving fast because it's late. Don't worry, I'm used to these roads." The jeep swerved squealing wildly at another turn in the road. Luckily, there was nothing else coming from the opposite direction – obviously Jhargram shut down early for the night or perhaps it was under tiger curfew. Then, clearly under the squealing wheels, Rohan heard the tinkle of what sounded like a cycle bell. Ganesh must have heard it too because he swerved even more wildly to avoid the bicycle he thought was coming and the jeep seemed to lose all contact with the road, hitting a bump and jumping into the air.

Rohan heard Ganesh curse and saw him wrenching at the brake – not that that was going to be of much use. The jeep bounded forward like a wild thing over the ditch that bordered the road and landed with a bone-shaking jerk on the uneven ground and then, slowly, began to topple over. Rohan had his seatbelt on but Ganesh like most night drivers hadn't bothered with it. As the jeep toppled, he went flying out and then the jeep fell.

Rohan, strapped into his seat stayed put, but his phone was not so lucky and went flying out of his pocket – he heard it crash. Once the jeep was still, he spent some time trying to figure out how to get out of the seat without damaging anything. Bablu Mama's caretaker was absolutely silent and he was worried about him but perhaps his phone would be intact. Carefully he unstrapped himself with one hand, hanging onto the side strap with the other so that he wouldn't topple. Having manoeuvred himself so that he could sit on the upturned edge of his seat, he managed to climb out of the door on his side, thankful that he was wearing jeans and not shorts. Then he dropped down and went round the jeep to look at Ganesh.

He was out cold but luckily only the upper part of the jeep had fallen on his legs, so he was wedged between that and the doorframe. Rohan tried to feel for his heart and thought he heard him breathe. With a sigh of relief, he went searching for Ganesh's phone. All he found was his own which refused to switch on. There was absolute darkness all around. What he needed to do was find a village. Taking a deep breath and hoping that there were no snakes in the bush, he started to walk, wishing for a torch, wishing for his phone, wishing... He didn't like leaving Ganesh there, but he couldn't free him from the jeep and waiting around wouldn't help if he was seriously injured. He had spent a night in the wild in the Sunderbans – and despite all the tigers, nothing had happened, though yes he wasn't alone – but he was certain he could do the same thing here. Well not that certain, but hopeful.

As he walked, he was unconsciously waiting to hear the yap of a dog, but there was none instead, all at once, there was something that he thought was a jackal's howl. He stopped wishing he had a torch and waiting to hear it again – he had heard them often enough on the lawns of the Tolly Club in Kolkata, beyond the dark horizon of the golf course fringed by trees, a symphony of jackals howling in winter; first, a lone howl and then gradually, a chorus. In the wild, packs of jackals often tracked tigers hoping to find their kills – the fact that they were around meant that there could be a tiger kill nearby.

A howl sounded almost in his ear and he started. He saw eyes in the shadows not so far away – first one pair, and then a ring of them further back just where the shadows became even darker.

He stood still and waited. The howls became a chorus. With his feet, he began feeling cautiously for stones in the grass. If he could pick up a few and throw them, the jackals might run away. Then he heard something else moving through the bushes – the eyes began to retreat until suddenly they had disappeared. Firefly flashes began and he saw, strangely against all hope, the silhouette of a man. "Sir!" escaped from his lips like a sigh of relief and he fell on his knees in the prickly grass.

6

here's a problem!" Rohan told Carpet Sahib. "The jeep overturned. Bablu Mama's caretaker is trapped."

"Where were you walking through the jungle?" In all their encounters, Carpet Sahib had never spoken aloud but Rohan could hear him very clearly over the chirping cicadas – it was how he had always been since that first encounter with the tiger that had escaped from Corbett National Park.

"I was looking for help. The phones have crashed." He could feel a certain amount of impatience in Carpet Sahib's aura. "So you left him lying there with jackals all around! There's no time to waste." Rohan could feel Carpet Sahib summoning something or someone. Soon afterwards, the bushes began to stir and a pair of eyes glowed in the darkness.

"The tiger!" Rohan cried. There was an instant growl. Carpet Sahib stood between the eyes and Rohan. "He'll take us to the jeep. I don't think you will be able to find him. And we have to hurry."

Carpet Sahib and the tiger moved soundlessly through the bushes, the tiger loping ahead of Carpet Sahib's glide, leaving Rohan to scuttle after them. He kept looking out for snakes and jumping over ditches, just about managing not to fall down, though he stumbled on a few occasions and wished he had a torch. He hadn't thought about the jackals, he had been so intent on finding help. "I understand why you did what you did, boy," he could hear Carpet Sahib saying. "But think things through sometimes."

Rohan was scratched all over by the time they reached the jeep. He could hear Ganesh groaning, which meant that he was beginning to recover his consciousness. The tiger was prowling restlessly round the groaning man, looking enquiringly at Carpet Sahib from time to time. "How can we move the jeep?" Rohan wanted to know. "Can the tiger push it over?"

He felt Carpet Sahib laughing. "Tigers can do a lot of things, but wrestling with overturned jeeps is beyond them. If there were two, we could think of something." He was silent for a while. Listening to the caretaker groaning, Rohan hoped that he had not opened his eyes and seen the tiger. Ganesh certainly would have been shocked into a heart attack. Then Carpet Sahib was on the move again. "I'll be back," he told Rohan. "You stay here. And if you see jackals, clap your hands and shout. "

Rohan sat next to Ganesh trying to feel brave. He had been in this situation before, he told himself but never with a wounded man in a jungle. Of course, the only tiger for miles around was being taken care of by Carpet Sahib but strange things like wolves, or even hyenas, came out of forests at times. To distract himself from all the rustles in the bushes, he carefully tiptoed around the jeep looking for a water bottle. There would be one in his backpack. He found that his backpack had hit the roof of the jeep so that was easy enough to get to it without disturbing the jeep. Pulling out the water bottle he went to Ganesh and splashed some water on his face. Ganesh's eyes were still shut but he opened his mouth and his tongue went feeling for the water and licked at it. Rohan drew back and waited. Something rustled in the bushes, and he saw eyes glowing again. His heart leapt uncomfortably and he shouted. The eyes disappeared.

Glancing at his watch he saw that it was not that late – 10.30, which by Kolkata standards was early. His mother would be making him practice equations for another half hour. But by Jhargram standards, it was possibly midnight. He looked sadly at his broken phone and wondered how to tell his mother and the uncles that he was all right. He couldn't hear Ganesh's phone ringing so that had obviously been broken in the crash too.

Suddenly he heard a crashing and trampling among the bushes. The trees began to shake and something huge and definitely no ghost came out of the trees. For a moment, he was terrified scrambling back towards the jeep. Then the moving shadows took the shape of an elephant. "Move away from there," he heard Carpet Sahib say. "We've got help in lifting the jeep." Rohan looked around for

him and then thought that he was possibly on the elephant's back – it was too dark to be sure. There were no signs of the tiger though. The elephant came forward and curled its trunk through the window on the other side. It strained and the jeep lifted a few inches with creaks of metal parts. It strained again, backing into the bushes and this time the jeep lifted some more. "See if you can pull that man out," Carpet Sahib told Rohan. "Carefully though, he may have broken something."

Rohan went to the other side of the jeep and the elephant held the vehicle's frame suspended in mid-air for long enough for Rohan to pull Ganesh's legs clear. It took some effort and at every moment Rohan was afraid that the jeep would come crashing down again. By the time he had pulled the caretaker clear, he was dripping with sweat. The elephant let the jeep go again and it thudded down on the grass. Ganesh groaned and tried to move, though his eyes were still shut.

The elephant's trunk reached out again and it picked Ganesh up and set him over its back. "Your turn next," Carpet Sahib said. To his surprise,

Rohan found the trunk curling around his waist. He was lifted off the ground and the elephant dumped him behind its ears. He could feel Ganesh sprawled behind him and hoped that he would not fall off. "This elephant has no howdah?" Rohan asked, sounding jittery. "No, it's a wild elephant come down from the hills but don't worry, he'll go carefully." Carpet Sahib assured him, reading his thoughts.

With a lurch, the elephant began to move. For such a huge creature, it moved very softly through the trees with none of the crashes that Rohan had heard before. Except at one point it stopped and yanked at something, causing Rohan to grab at a flapping ear while trying to clutch Ganesh behind him. "Camera trap," he heard the voice say. "Elephants hate camera traps and we don't need one to record this right now."

"Where are we going?" Rohan asked. "To Bablu Mama's bungalow?"

Carpet Sahib laughed, "I don't know where that is, but the elephant's taking us to a *chai* stall.

You'll find people there. He can smell the sugar they use."

However, what was Rohan going to say when a wild elephant dropped him and Ganesh off, he had no idea. Clutching to the elephant's swaying back, he began thinking about it.

7

The situation in Kolkata was tense. Rohan wasn't answering his phone and his mother finally managed to contact the caretaker's wife only to discover that the caretaker hadn't come home either. "The tiger's eaten them," the hysterical wife declared, which upset Rohan's mother all the more. She was about to call Rohan's father in Dubai but the Khan Sahib and the Major stopped her. They were convinced that something had happened on the road. "After all, he called to say that he had arrived and was with the caretaker, didn't he?"

"You mean they met the tiger?" Rohan's mother demanded.

The Major and the Khan Sahib looked at each other; and Khan Sahib quickly lowered his gaze to his glass and rattled the ice around in it. They had never told Rohan's parents about his brushes with tigers and leopards. "We should probably try to leave for Jhargram tonight," the Major said, more to reassure Rohan's mother that something was being done. "As for the tiger, it hasn't been seen in quite a while. Some fellow said he met it in Malda."

Met wasn't quite the right word. A man had come staggering into the centre of Malda with a clawed cheek and declared that the tiger had attacked him while he was checking his mango trees. The press had made a great fuss of the man, persuading him to show his cheek and ranting about what they called the most feared paws in the jungle had done. "Always hysterical the media," the Khan Sahib had commented. "Malda I gather is miles from Lalgarh. The tiger can't have covered that distance in a night."

The forest department officials announced that they would check the claw marks to determine what they belonged to and took the man to the government hospital. From there they announced that it was most probably a wolf that had attacked the man. "The most feared paws in the jungle," said the Khan Sahib to the Major, with a wry smile.

"We should contact the police!" Rohan's mother declared, deciding that the uncles lacked the proper sense of concern.

"Yesss," the Major agreed, "that may be a good idea."

A sleepy constable answered the phone at Binpur thana. He sounded even sleepier when he heard Rohan's mother's voice, so she handed the phone over to the Major. The Major stumbled through the conversation in a mix of English and Hindi but managed to get the caretaker's name across "Ganesh Mahato, *gayab ho giya jungle mein!*"

"Missing," hissed Rohan's mother. "Say missing."

"Missing," said the Major dutifully and repeated it.

Ultimately the message went through and the constable said that he would alert the night patrol. Roads were narrow and occasionally accidents did happen. There were also elephants coming down from the hills and they had been thinking of organizing a *hulla* party to drive the beasts away from the fields before someone got trampled.

Rohan's mother was horrified. "What kind of place has he gone to? Bablu didn't say it was like that!" She tried Rohan's phone again without any luck. The Major and the Khan Sahib escorted her home from the Club and waited with her. She tried Rohan's phone again without any luck. It was almost 1 a.m. when the phone rang. Rohan's mother snatched it up. "Hello, yes, *haanh!* Found him! Thank god! Caretaker hurt in an accident? I see…" She finally disconnected the line and slumped back in her chair.

"So he's been found?" the Khan Sahib prompted.

"Huh? Oh, yes. There was an accident. The caretaker's been hurt. My son managed to carry him to a tea stall… I think he should come home."

"Is Rohan all right?"

"Oh yes, the police said he was fine…"

"Let's think about this tomorrow," the Khan Sahib said. "You should go to bed and we'll be setting out for Midnapore. We can always see how Rohan is and bring him back. Don't worry – you know he is all right now. And there's no need to worry his father anymore." Rohan's mother had to agree.

ohan could not understand how he could just go up to a tea stall on the back of a wild elephant in the middle of the night. "Sir," he said. "How…"

"He's a light man. The elephant will put you down in the bushes and then you can carry him to the tea stall." Rohan hoped that he would be able to manage that. Ganesh had stopped groaning and seemed to be unconscious again. He clutched at the elephant's back instead of crossing his fingers. Like a well-trained domestic creature and not like a wild thing at all, the elephant kneeled down, though the sudden back and front sway almost sent Rohan flying and clutching behind him frantically to make sure that Ganesh did not fall off. Then the trunk reached back, curled around Rohan's waist, and set him down on the ground. It did the same thing with the caretaker. "See if you can pick him up," the voice in his head said to Rohan.

Rohan bit his lip and tried to figure out what the best way to do it was – ghosts obviously could not lift people. "Sling him over your back like a backpack. You might find that easier." Carpet Sahib was standing beside him looking down at Ganesh. "He's unconscious so that will be less trouble." After a few attempts, Rohan managed to sling Ganesh over his back – the caretaker was small and light so he was not too much of a weight.

"I will walk with you. There's a light ahead – can you see it?"

Rohan raised his head and saw a glimmer beyond the trees. "That's the tea stall. Go tell them about the jeep accident. There's nothing in the grass, don't worry."

Step by step, Rohan staggered forward through the tall grass and the bushes with the man on his back seeming to grow heavier at every step. Slowly the bushes thinned and finally he could see bamboo poles and a tin roof. There were men visible by the light of a bulb hanging from the roof and he could hear the buzz of conversation. "I have to leave you now," said the voice beside him. "Just keep walking." Rohan had the sense of being left alone before he had time to ask any further questions. He staggered forward until the light fell on him and then he shouted for help before falling flat on his face with Ganesh's weight on his back.

He heard feet scuffling around him and then the weight was taken from his back. "Arré, Ganesh! What has happened? Who's this?" They helped him sit up and shoved a steaming hot pot of tea into Rohan's hand. He sipped it and explained about the jeep crash.

Ganesh was laid carefully on a bench and Rohan was relieved to see that his eyelids were fluttering. One of the men was on the phone. "Arré constable, jeep accident. Ganesh serious!" Rohan, drowsing sleepily over his tea, wondered whether he had actually heard him say that. For that matter had he heard Carpet Sahib say, "See you in a while," or had he imagined that too?

"What? You already know? Achcha, the boy's mother called. Well you can tell her he's all right. I don't think he has a phone. Ganesh needs a doctor, I think… Night Patrol…let me ask the boy…" The man turned to Rohan, "Do you know the place where the jeep went off the road?"

Rohan shook his head. "I don't know the place, but there was a bump on the road."

The man nodded, "Oh, that hathi bump – we've telling the Public Works to lower it!" and went back to his conversation with the constable. When he had finished, he told Rohan, "The police will tell your Ma that you are safe. Where are you from? The city?" By city he meant Calcutta. "Yes," Rohan answered feeling very tired. "I came to stay at my Bablu Mama's bungalow."

"Sen Babu? You're Sen Babu's nephew?" The men at the tea stall looked at each other and nodded wisely. Obviously, they would know his uncle in a small area like that. "How are you feeling?"

"Very tired," Rohan answered, "but otherwise all right. Shouldn't you call Ganesh's wife?"

One of the men was feeling Ganesh's pulse. "Steady," he said. "But we should get him to the Doctor Babu. No, don't try to get up." Ganesh had been trying to raise his head. "You had an accident with the jeep…"

"Boy…" Ganesh mumbled.

"Boy brought you here. He probably saved your life." Ganesh struggled half way up this time and looked around wildly till he caught sight of Rohan. "Sen Babu," he muttered.

"He told us. Relax. The police are looking for your jeep. I'll call Shibur Ma and tell her." The man pushed Ganesh back down on the bench. "Want some tea? Or should I give you water?" He reached behind him, felt for a glass on the table and held it to Ganesh's lips. Ganesh drank and then lay back on the bench. "My head aches."

"The jeep fell on you," Rohan said. "You were very lucky."

"You must be some kind of *pehlwan* to get him out from under the jeep," another of the men said admiringly. "Do you gym a lot?"

"It was only the roof of the jeep next above the window," Rohan said. "And there was a rock that caught some of the weight." He thought it was better to add the rock story just in case – there was every chance that they might ask him to demonstrate his weightlifting skills."

He began to wish for a bed and some sort of food but just then he heard the sound of an engine and a jeep with a red light came to a halt in front of the tea stall. A policeman in khaki climbed out. *"Eichheley?* This the boy?" he asked with a jerk of his head. "We've found the jeep. You'll need to come and identify it."

Rohan drove off in the jeep – the *policewala* had an assistant with him who was very curious about the whole thing, what Rohan wanted to do in Jhargram and why. However, the moment he heard the word 'baagh', he lapsed into silence. "Can't be a real tiger," said his colleague. "Must be a bhoot." That word again, Rohan thought – as far as he knew, there was only one bhoot, though that was Manjul's term for the man who used to be Carpet Sahib. He thought Ghost Who Walks was a better description, even though it did belong to The Phantom. "Two people die looking for it but that's their own fault. No one else sees it for days. What say, boy?"

Boy agreed politely looking at the passing trees and the sudden flashes either of fireflies or animal's eyes. Once he heard a jackal howl. "The tiger's watchman," the cop at the wheel said. "Perhaps Baagh Mama is on the prowl." He stopped the jeep by the roadside and Rohan saw the crooked palm. The policeman flicked on his torch and the beam picked out the toppled jeep.

"My phone is somewhere and Ganesh's..." Rohan said, "And my backpack is in the back." The three of them got down and walked over to the jeep. Rohan noted that they had pistols in their belts, though whether they would stop anything larger than a jackal was doubtful. They also wore boots, presumably for snake protection.

Rohan managed to fish his backpack out and by the light of the torch, they found his and Ganesh's phones. The torchlight also showed Rohan what he had not seen before, a dark pool of petrol.

"You're lucky, boy! No fires! And look here…" the torchlight fell on a trampled bush a little further away. "Hathi! Very lucky boy – go home and do Ganesh Puja! Now let's get out of here before something else comes along."

"Where are you taking me?" Rohan asked wondering if he was going to spend a night in the thana.

"To Sen Babu's bungalow. We have told his wife."

There would be various kinds of police procedure, reporting the accident and other things, but they said that could be done next morning. When they got to the tea stall, Ganesh was sitting up and cursing the 'hathi bump' that he had hit. He didn't want to have anything to do with doctors and hospitals but since the police were involved, they would need an official statement that everything was fine. One of the policemen bent close to him and sniffed up and down while the men laughed. Didn't they have breathalysers in Jhargram? Rohan wondered.

"*Dhat*!" Ganesh spluttered. "I heard that Master Moshai's cycle bell and thought I was going to hit him! So I swerved."

"That Maoist! And out at night!"

"He takes tuition in the evening," someone said quickly. "The constable's son." When they heard that whatever tension there was in the atmosphere evaporated. Ganesh quickly felt up and down his kurta, produced the bungalow keys and announced that he was ready to go home.

The jeep dropped them outside the gate of Bablu Mama's bungalow, waited while Ganesh opened the padlock and closed it again behind them. Ganesh limped over the pebbled drive towards the front door. "There is a landline in the bungalow," he told Rohan. "You can call your mother from there."

The bungalow's door opened, a woman came out and burst into a shower of abuse when she saw Ganesh but then, catching sight of Rohan, she quietened down. Bath and bed, Rohan thought that was all he wanted. "And all the things I cooked for the young babu getting cold," the woman, who was Shibu's Ma he gathered, mourned, while glaring at her husband from time to time, "Rich mutton curry, a little rice…"

"I don't want to eat anything right now," Rohan said. He didn't even want to phone his mother, but knew he had to, so he dialled her number sleepily from the landline told he was all right and would talk to her tomorrow. Then he fell into his bed and was soon asleep.

He thought he would be too tired to dream, but he found himself walking across the dark grass of what looked like the Khan Sahib's back garden. He could hear the jackals howling in chorus. He remembered the Khan Sahib saying that his grandfather would have stalked into his gunroom, pulled down a Purdey and fired several rounds into the trees, leaving the sweepers to pick up dead jackals before dawn so that any visitors were not disturbed. There always were dead jackals. Looking into his glass, the Khan Sahib laughed, "My grandfather could shoot sound accurately, hitting a bell dangling from a branch blindfolded. He tried to teach me to do that."

Rohan glanced down and suddenly saw that the grass beside him bending and then a tiger's paw print formed and vanished, formed and vanished. There was a tiger walking beside him but he could not see it, just the grass moving. The jackal howls fell silent. "You're playing a game," a voice said. "It's called hunt the tiger."

9

The caretaker's wife was full of stories. She brought Rohan 'rumble-tumble' for breakfast without asking him and put a fat banana on the table beside it. The eggs were stringy but had lots of butter with liberally sprinkled pepper, so he ate and sneezed. Shibur Ma stood by the table looking out into the garden, and Rohan decided it might be nice to tell her how good the eggs were in case it improved her cooking. She turned and her face lit up. "Really? I don't make this *ingreji* stuff unless Sen Babu comes down."

"How is Ganesh this morning? *Thikthak?*" Rohan asked through a mouthful of egg.

She made a face. "He will have to go see the doctor. His middle is very painful and he has a big black bruise all the way up his back. Thank you for saving his life Choto Babu. If he'd been left lying in the jungle, the jackals would have got him."

"How is it you didn't say *tiger*?" Rohan asked curiously. "And no one has seen it in a long time."

She snorted, "52 villages in this region worship *bondebota*. Every five years the Adivasi people get together at the end of March and offer puja to him. So the *debota* agrees that there will be no *hamla* for five years until the contract is renewed."

Rohan had heard about villages making contracts with tigers – the Sunderbans had their shamans and there was a famous tiger whisperer who would drive a nail into a deodar tree trunk for every contract that he made with a tiger. In return, the tiger was expected to come and drag his claws over the nail as a kind of signature. This had kept the village safe for decades until a particularly treacherous tiger came along. The tiger had met the whisperer, shaken its shaggy head in agreement and dragged its claws across the nail after the metal head was hammered in. Certain that everything was secure, the whisperer had returned to his hut and gone about pounding herbs in his pestle and mortar and muttering mantras. In the evening, as was his custom, he left his hut to go to the pond and draw water for his evening cooking. Everyone saw him go, but he never returned. The setting sun stained the sky the colour of blood and darkness fell blotting out all the light. It was an uneasy kind of darkness – everyone in the village later swore that they had felt something wrong but though they lit fires outside their homes and wondered where the whisperer was, no one had the courage to go look for him.

The women found him sprawled by the pond the next morning with a tiger's claw marks across his body. From that day on, the village made no more contracts with tigers.

"Superstition," Rohan heard Ganesh's voice say. Ganesh dragged himself to the table and plopped down into a chair. "There is no tiger."

"How can you say that?" his wife asked. "Paw prints, someone injured...*oi jey Gopinath bolechilo* – he said he saw a tiger slightly bigger than a calf."

"After a glass of moonshine, Murmu will say anything!" Ganesh said. "If there was a baagh, would that stupid schoolmaster go cycling through the forest to give tuition at night? And make me crash the jeep into the bargain! *Na na* the Maoists are spreading stories about tigers to keep people away from what they are actually doing. It's just a cooked up story!" His wife slopped a cup of tea in front of him and he sipped it. Then he turned to Rohan, "There's no jeep and I will have to go to see the doctor and then the *poliss* people. I am sorry Choto Babu, I don't know what you will do. Perhaps you should go home?"

"And why should he go home?" the wife demanded. "If there is no tiger, there is no trouble. He can go wherever he likes. There's the old cycle in the *garridge*. Choto Babu, can you cycle?"

"Yes," Rohan said, nodding vigorously.

"Then there's no problem. And how are you going to the doctor?" she asked her husband. "Choto Babu can't carry you there the way he carried you to the tea stall."

"I'll call a cycle rickshaw. Thank goodness, Sen Babu insisted on keeping the landline. Your phone must be out of charge anyway."

Rohan got to his feet and asked to see the bicycle. It was old but the tyres were fine and he rode it a few times round the garden with the caretaker's wife watching him anxiously. "Which way shall I go?" he asked her.

"Wherever you like," she said. "The Rajbari is that side and the jungle is all around. Or, if you like ghost stories…" Rohan pricked his ears at the word 'bhoot' "…you can go to Ram Swarup Baba's ashram in Laljal. It's probably his tiger's ghost that people are seeing. You might also see the Baba's bhoot if you're lucky."

She wasn't able to give him directions to Laljal— which turned out to be in another administrative block. Rohan's fingers itched for his phone – he could have found the place through his GPS. However, he took the cycle outside the gate and began his rickety ride down the roads. He thought he could find his way back to the tea stall and find out how to get to Laljal.

He cycled past cows and curious children who waved at him. "Which way is Laljal?" he asked them hopefully and they pointed towards the forest. "But don't go there," they added. "There's a tiger." Finally, he did manage to find the tea stall. The owner recognized him. "Laljal? It's a long ride. But it's only nine o' clock, perhaps you'll be able to go and make it back before dark." From somewhere, he pulled out a tea-stained map. "Lots of tourists come looking for forts. Here, take this. But turn back if you think you will be getting late."

Just as Rohan was turning to get back on his bicycle, the man stopped him again. "You don't have a phone, no? Take this one." He held out a small phone. "Ganesh is a friend and you helped him last night. It's topped up and charged so it will take you to Laljal and back." Rohan could not refuse. He needed a phone and he hoped this one had GPS.

As soon as the tea stall was out of sight, he stopped and checked the phone. There was GPS and he entered his location and Laljal. The phone was slow but it managed to show him a route. Following that, he began cycling. Luckily, barring a stray truck or a jeep, the roads were empty. The low hanging trees looked the same and he wondered how people found their way. Sometimes he would catch a gleam of water through the fields and occasionally the land behind the road sloped down.

He realized that getting to Laljal would take quite a lot of cycling and began wondering when he would run into a tea stall. To distract himself, he turned off the road and began to follow a track through the trees. Tracks were always promising – they led to villages and tea stalls which might be better than following a road with lorries and jeeps and besides there was always the hope of a tiger.

Some of the trees had red berries and others dangled strings of flowers like pearls. A squirrel scuttled up a trunk and turned to insult Rohan in a stream of chittering. It was almost like being in the forests around Nainital again, no sound except for twitters and the squirrel's outrage. Except all at once Rohan heard shouts and the crashing of bushes. A lot of people and the way the shouts were moving they were on the track of something – the tiger? He wheeled the bicycle to the tree trunk and kept his back to it and his face to the voices and the noise.

The trees were moving as something passed beneath them. No, not tiger but… an elephant burst through the bushes and was looking straight at Rohan. A stone flew after it and hit its back. It flinched and raised its trunk trumpeting in rage. Rohan walked towards it with his heart in his mouth. The elephant's ears flapped and it raised its trunk while the shouts and another stone thudded on its back. Then the wind blew to the elephant from the boy, and for a moment it looked at Rohan and its flapping ears slowed. Rohan ran up to it shouting, "Hup! Hup!" hoping it would get the message before the people came out of the bushes – and he could hear the sounds of their feet getting louder.

It looked at him considerately and the redness in the restless eyes faded slightly. It reached out with its trunk, raised Rohan in the air and placed him behind his ears just as the people burst out with their stones and sticks. Then it turned to face the mob that now saw the boy on the elephant's back. "*Eh kee*! Was he there before?" Sticks and stones raised they stared.

"What has my elephant done?" Rohan demanded.

"Your elephant? He's wild!"

"No, he just runs away…" the mob was advancing seeing that the elephant wasn't doing anything. Rohan didn't like it at all. He wished frantically for Carpet Sahib but realized that this was not the right situation. The elephant's ears were flapping and hitting his legs and the back was shifting and twitching. At any moment, he thought, he would fall off. Trying to grip the elephant's back with his knees, he whipped out his phone, "Hi constable! Sen Babu's nephew Rohan here. Yes, everything is all right. I have found my hathi but…" Rodeo rider flashed into his head as he tried to keep his balance on the swaying back – because the elephant was swaying restlessly. At the word 'constable', the mob began backing and some of the stones plopped onto the ground.

The elephant raised its trunk and trumpeted, its movements echoing that of the crowd. "In a minute," Rohan thought, "he will be back onto the road and we'll get run over by a truck! Stop!" he cried aloud. "*Thamo!*" There was a sharp crack like a gunshot and the elephant swerved and charged towards the trees and the running people, with Rohan clutching frantically at its ears.

Khan Sahib and the Major descended at a bustling station filled with people going about their early morning business. Someone was building a cage with sal stakes in one corner, a woman was selling marigolds for puja, hot jalebis were being fried, and both men agreed that the aroma was delicious. The Major began fumbling for loose change in his pockets when the Khan Sahib nudged him. "Look there." The Major looked. Arrows were on sale along with bows made from bendy sal wood. They didn't look like toys. The Major caught an official-looking man in khaki who was probably the station master and asked in Hindi, "What are those for?"

The Station Master hardly glanced at them "Shikar Utsav," he said and added in English,

"Hunting Festival." Outside the station there were even more stalls. One was selling spears with wooden handles and sharp heads. "Where have we come to!" the Major exclaimed. "Does the forest department know about all this?" A jeep was waiting for them and the moment they climbed in, the Major asked the driver, "Do you know about this Shikar Utsav?"

"*Ji*, sahib," answered the driver starting the jeep. "It happens every year at this time. It is one of the *parabas* or festivals of the tribes that live here. They hunt in honour of Bondebota." They passed a truck with its radio belting out Hindi film songs and a bunch of excited young men with scarves tied round their heads. "When the Maoists were here, it had stopped, but now it has been celebrated again for quite a few years." The driver added hastily, "The forest department knows of course." He knew these sahibs were important forest people and he didn't want to lose his job.

It was still quite early in the morning when the train had drawn into the station. The village pundit was in the fields with his sacred thread twisted around his ear. He was tired of being told not to go out for his morning business, so he had decided to risk it. Everyone in their village was convinced the tiger was a Maoist plot anyway. Comfortably squatting behind a bush with the breeze from the trees on his back, the pundit was happy and content. But then, he heard a noise – nothing that sounded like a tiger but a tractor motor kind of noise that seemed to be coming from somewhere above him. Something whizzed overhead. The pundit blinked the sun out of his eyes and tried to follow it. A toy airplane, he thought disgustedly and went back to the village to report. Habu who was bringing the cows back from a walk round the nearest field heard him. "Drone!" he announced importantly.

"*Kee*? These boys think they know everything!" the pundit snorted.

"He's probably right," said the Pradhan. "The forest department has sent it flying to see if they can spot the tiger."

"Among all that tangle of trees? *Pagol*! They must be mad!" Then a thought struck the pundit, "You think they could see me?"

"Very possibly," the Pradhan answered gravely and went back to his newspaper.

The drones did not pick up any tigers on their morning flight, and apart from the pundit behind the bush, they did send back an astonishing image of a boy on the back of a wild elephant – a remarkably clear image.

The Khan Sahib, who was relaxing in the Rajbari with the Major, was sent the image by the forest department. The two had spent the morning recovering from the worries of losing Rohan by enjoying the sights and sounds of the Shikar Utsav, walking through the garden and verandahs, and then ending up in the billiards room and looking at the tigers and buffaloes shot by the previous zamindars mounted on the walls. "We started the rot," the Khan Sahib said. "Tiger hunts for the collectors... proving what heroes we were and thinking god would provide never-ending tiger skins for our walls, all of them longer than eight feet when you stretched them out."

"My grandfather had a thing for elephants," the Major said. "He turned their feet into stools."

The uncles had a language problem. Communication was carried out in fragments of Hindi and English. They had hoped to bring Rohan over as soon as possible and his mother had handed the Khan Sahib a replacement phone for him. When they phoned the bungalow, they heard a woman at the other end saying that Rohan had gone cycling and her husband had gone to the hospital – or so their translator told them. Therefore, they phoned the forest department instead. By noon they had the pictures of Rohan on the back of the elephant. "Tigers! Elephants! That boy!" the Major exploded.

"How do we track him down?" the Khan Sahib demanded. Then he relaxed. "Best not to tell the boy's mother. Unless… is the media going to release this?"

Joydip Babu from the forest department shook his head, "Not if we do not release this footage. What we can do is send out our hulla party to flush out elephants and make sure that the villagers don't get to them."

"And if the tiger gets in the way?"

Joydip Babu looked at his colleague – he had brought a young woman with him dressed in a dull brown salwar kameez with sneakers on her feet. "This is my colleague Purabi Mahato," Joydip said. "She is the Additional Forest Officer and has promised to talk to the tribals. Their Shikar Utsav is around the corner."

"Yes," the Khan Sahib said. "We saw the people outside the station."

"They hunt," Purabi explained, "and sacrifice to Bonodebota, the god of the forests. I have been talking to the Pradhans to ensure that they explain matters to the villagers." She had long black hair and wide eyes and there was an intensity in her expression that reminded the Khan Sahib of a girl he knew back in Uttarkhand. Manjul had wanted to come with them, but there was no way that could have been possible. She had the cows to look after, classes, term examinations and wary parents. This girl – well he had heard that she was the Additional Forest Office and she was apparently quite experienced – was looking at him with the same eagerness. He wondered whether the Major thought the same.

"The other problem is that the elephants have destroyed the camera traps. They tend to smell them out," Joydip said.

"Can we go to the police station first?" the Khan Sahib asked. "I think it would be wise to warn the local authorities about the hunt. We saw the preparations around the station this morning. If the forest department doesn't have men to patrol, that is?"

"An emotional approach works better Khan Sahib," Purabi said confidently. "I belong to one of their tribes. The authorities have harassed the locals enough when the Maoists were on the prowl. Please leave this to us."

However, the Khan Sahib and the Major insisted on going to the police station, so Joydip Babu and Purabi accompanied them. The police in Binpur were delighted to meet the burra sahibs from the North and even happier to discover that they knew Rohan. "That boy is a hero!" one of the police officers declared. "He saved Ganesh's life. And that too when an elephant was trampling around in the area!"The uncles exchanged glances at that – if they knew Rohan, there had to be some connection with that elephant. However, the hunt was of more importance so they brought it up, only to have the police assuring them that the adivasis were harmless people, the hunt was just a custom and no one ever got hurt.

They then went to the village in the forest department jeep. The villagers came up to stare at the Major and the Khan Sahib because they looked like outsiders and they stood in the centre of an uncomfortable circle until the Pradhan came up and greeted them. He spoke in Hindi for the benefit of the outsiders but the conversation switched almost immediately to the local dialect.

Someone brought stools for the Khan Sahib and the Major and clay *bhars* or pots of tea were put into their hands. They sat down to watch what was happening.

Joydip and the girl began what looked like an intense conversation carried out at top speed. Hands waved, heads were shaken. The villagers occasionally chimed in with a *Hoonh* and a *Haanh* while the Pradhan managed to look serious and dignified. After a while, he summoned some elderly villagers to come up behind him while the conversation continued.

Then the girl suddenly flung herself down at their feet, with elaborate pranam then sitting cross-legged in the dust and looking up at the Pradhan and the elders. Her voice rose and fell dramatically. The village elders looked suitably moved by the plea and nodded their heads. The girl then got to her feet, joined her hands together in a namaste and walked back to where the Major and the Khan Sahib were seated. "Should we go?" she asked, brushing the dust off her khaki kurta.

They returned to the jeep. The girl explained what she had said to the Major and Khan Sahib in a brief outline. "I think it was effective," she added.

"Do you have any plans for capturing the tiger?" the Khan Sahib asked.

"We'll have to get it to the village," Joydip said. "Then we can net it."

"But wouldn't the presence of people be more complicated?" the Major wanted to know. "Couldn't you just track it and dart it? Some of these villagers must be expert trackers."

The girl and Joydip exchanged looks. "Actually we're better at manoeuvring tigers in villages. That works very well in the Sunderbans."

From what the Khan Sahib and the Major had seen of Jhargram, it looked very like Kumaon – plains and undulating hills with dry dusty embankments and open spaces. "If you have a dart gun," the Major said, "I can help you track the tiger."

The two Forest officials shook their heads. "Thank you, that's very kind, but we understand these people and it would be easier for us to deal with it. Can we help you track the boy and the elephants?"

"The trouble is," said the Major later, "We didn't understand what the girl was saying."

She seemed to have been humble, entreating the Pradhan, folding her hands and then of course humbling herself in the dust. "Sometimes dramatics work," the Khan Sahib observed. "In the meantime, we have to find that boy. Elephants can make people disappear sometimes. Remember Ashok?" He was a researcher they had worked with who had stumbled across a herd of elephants while exploring the forest on foot. The party had had a jeep with them but decided it would be less disturbing for the deer they were tracking if they walked. So they left the jeep on the main road and happily meandered through the forest only to find their way suddenly blocked by an elephant. It was followed by other members of the herd and in their hurry to escape the group of researchers was separated. When they reassembled, Ashok was missing.

The uncles were young at the time and hadn't known what to do – Ashok had a wife and they couldn't quite tell her that they had lost him to a herd of elephants. They sat with the others in the forest bungalow biting their nails and sending out telegrams asking for advice. Ashok sheepishly turned up two days later, saying that he had lost his way and would have stayed lost if he hadn't stumbled on a wandering cowherd.

"He's been lost before," the Khan Sahib said. "And it isn't tigers this time, it's only an elephant. Let's wait." Though both he and the Major had a guilty conscience about that.

abu was reluctantly on his way to school dragging his school bag in the dust when he ran into Budai-er Ma. She had a polythene packet in one hand and looked as happy as a bird. "Oh Habu!" she called when she saw him. "Come here…" Anything, he thought to delay the first history class! "What's up Mashi?" he asked.

She fumbled in the packet and pulled out a fat yellow laddoo, which she shoved into his mouth. It was almost too big for his mouth, but Habu was fond of laddoos and he adjusted his jaws and began munching. "Had some good news?" he asked with the laddoo tucked into one cheek.

"You know that old cow of mine? The one that had stopped giving milk and wasn't even eating any more?" Habu nodded. "Well, I sold it today!"

Habu almost choked on the laddoo but managed to control his breathing. "You sold it?" he gasped, taking the half-eaten sticky laddoo out of his mouth. No one in their right senses would have bought a cow on its last leg like that. Budai-er Ma gestured behind her. "Oi, oi, that fellow who calls himself Danda. He said the cow was perfect for him."

Habu popped the disintegrating laddoo back into his mouth and licked his sticky fingers. A fly was already buzzing around him. "Thank you!" he said, remembering his manners. "I have to go to school now." But he didn't take the direct path to school. He went around with Budai-er Ma taking the longer track that led round the village. He was curious about why anyone should want to buy an old cow – especially since the cow in question was all wrinkled skin and bones – he remembered seeing the animal standing sadly in her cattle shed with her head hanging low. "You're inquisitive about everything except studies," his mother had told him once, boxing his ear. Studies, he thought, were for girls – they had all the time in the world to read while watching the rice cook or working out sums when they went to the bazaar – the trouble was, most people didn't seem to agree with him.

He saw the men in conversation sitting among the trees a little way off the path. The cow was tethered to a branch and was listlessly grazing at the thin grass. It was grazing ground for a goat, not for a cow! Habu thought indignantly. He recognized the men – they waved at him and went on with their conversation. One of them was whittling at a stone and shaping something. Hansda was a good carver, making little statues that he would sell at the bus terminus or to tourists at the Rajbari. "What are you making?" he asked.

"Arrowheads, buddhu!" Hansda answered, his fingers busily shaping the rock. Arrowheads? Oh yes, the hunt. Habu picked up one of the finished arrowheads and tested the tip on his finger. "It's sharp!"

"Has to be. How will you kill anything otherwise?"

"What are you planning to kill?" Habu asked.

"Well, t…" he stopped himself. "Whatever Bondebota brings us."

"You were going to say tiger," Habu said accusingly.

"And what if I was? Bloody nuisance, stopping us collecting wood and grazing the cattle." He went back to his whiz-whiz-whiz shaping of the arrowheads while the other man leaned back against the tree and watched.

Habu knew that the bows for the arrows were carefully stored in the haylofts safe and dry from any chance of damp. They only came out on ceremonial occasions, when the strings were changed and tightened. Some of them were beautifully carved but nothing had been shot with them except for a few deer and once, by accident, a goat, which had triggered a village feud that went on for days. The police had almost been called in but because it was too soon after the Red terror, the village elders had ordered an end to it and the owner of the goat was given a new one by the hunter responsible.

Habu told Master Moshai what had happened when he got into class and Master Moshai looked very grave. "Don't tell anyone else," he told Habu. "The forest department has to know."

All that happened was a woman came in to do *buk-buk* with the Pradhan and various other pradhans from the surrounding villages in the early evening. She had some other forest *officewalas* with her, two of whom only spoke Hindi. She sat in the dust in front of the pradhans and said, "I am one of you and beg you not to hunt any animals in the forest this season. You know that there is a tiger on the loose. We are trying to trap it. Then you can do whatever you like in the forest. Bondebota will be pleased."

The rest of the village was eavesdropping on the conversation and Habu saw one or two of the men look shiftily at each other. He didn't like that look, but he was also getting fed up of cycling round and round the village for entertainment instead of running through the forests with his cows before school. "A tiger pelt can be sold for over twenty thousand," someone else muttered nearby, "provided, it is undamaged."

Habu, on the other hand, was thinking not about what the woman had to say – he hadn't really paid attention – but what he had heard. If a tiger was killed with arrows, how could the pelt remain undamaged then, Habu wondered. But since the pradhans were listening to the woman, perhaps they would forbid the hunt – who knew? He could still hear the grinding whiz-whiz-whiz sound of the arrowheads being sharpened.

12

The elephant lurched and trampled through the trees like a runaway train. Once it went straight through a cowshed and Rohan just escaped being brushed off by the thatch. Occasionally, he wondered whether elephants had brakes and how to apply them but most often he was too busy just staying on it. They did not pass too many people, though they did go through the outskirts of villages and through fields trampling the long grasses – or perhaps they were crops. They splashed through a shallow stream and into thick forest. He ducked just in time as they went under a low hanging branch and the monkeys in the trees shouted rude things after them. That was when Rohan felt the elephant beginning to slow down. It finally came to a gradual stop, its sides heaving.

Rohan looked around – they were in a grove with trees all around. The only sound was the twitter of birds and the occasional ringing of cicadas. Under him, the elephant's back shifted slightly. Then, without warning, the animal's hindquarters went down sharply as it sat down and Rohan almost slid off, saving himself by clinging to the ears. Not that an Indian elephant's ears gave much hold – if it had been African, perhaps then… The front went down with a thump and Rohan was on the level. Was he supposed to get off? The elephant's trunk curled back feeling for him. He realised that he was meant to get down and moved himself to where the elephant's shoulder should be, got his leg over and allowed himself to drop on the soft forest floor.

The first thing he did was feel for the phone and call his mother while the elephant regarded him curiously with those wise eyes that were no longer red with rage. He lied like a rug to his mother, "I'm fine, Ma. I've gone on a picnic. No, there's no tiger around. No, I haven't met the Khan Sahib or the Major. Ganesh has gone to the police station and then to see a doctor – or perhaps it's the other way round. No, I haven't had time to do any homework!" Of course I wouldn't, he thought, looking indignantly at the phone. How could she even think that it was possible? "A tea stall man gave me this phone," he added, "so you can get me on this number. Yes it's topped up and charged." And he hoped that the tea stall man wouldn't think that he had disappeared with the phone! News of his being kidnapped by an elephant was bound to spread like wildfire.

He looked around and now the excitement was over, he realized he was feeling hungry. The elephant had lumbered to its feet and was tearing leaves from one of the trees and was feeding itself. All very well for you! Isn't there any fruit handy?"

A figure stepped out from behind one of the trees and smiled. "Sir!" Rohan cried. "I should have known."

"Well you wanted to come to Laljal, didn't you?" Carpet Sahib asked.

"Is the tiger here?"

Carpet Sahib nodded. "Yes, this way. Slowly, though. He's a very edgy cat." The three of them — the elephant had joined them too — walked through the sunlight and shadows. The sunbeams were getting longer — it was afternoon, though still early. Rohan's feet were the only things making any noise and he was afraid that his stomach would start rumbling next.

It was not an easy path. Things slithered away in the undergrowth and there were thorny bushes that had to be avoided. Pebbles got under Rohan's sneakers and almost sent him flying. It seemed to be a never ending trail. "We're taking the long way," he heard Carpet Sahib say. "We don't want you and the elephant to run into any people."

All the while, the shadows grew longer. Rohan's phone rang once, "Yes, Ma. I'm still at…*Kantapahar* or somewhere. Yes Ma…" He could see Carpet Sahib's shoulders shaking with silent laughter. They continued to move. Rohan found a squishy bar of chocolate in his pocket and munched that — it was better than nothing. He should have listened to Ganesh's wife and brought some sandwiches or even 'chop cutlet' from the tea stall.

A deer came out of a sal thicket, looked at them with cocked head, then stopped to graze, unalarmed by Rohan or the elephant. No tiger, Rohan thought. It wouldn't behave like that if there were a tiger.

They came to a rocky outcrop and what looked like a hill rose steeply beyond. There was a path that skirted the hill and they took that, though it as overgrown with weeds. "People used to come this way on pilgrimage," Carpet Sahib said. "Their feet have made that path." Half hidden by bushes was a cave so carefully camouflaged that most people would overlook it. Carpet Sahib stopped at the entrance. Rohan peered into the darkness. He could smell damp fur.

There was a rumble like distant thunder from inside. Rohan hesitated. Then Carpet Sahib carefully stepped between Rohan and the mouth of the cave. "He's eaten — a wild pig. That's inside with him. After dark, we'll have to move him out of this region. He can't be left alone."

The tiger had got into a culvert and the forest department had sent men with fishing nets to trap him. They had put the nets at either end but the

men were either new or just terrified – when the infuriated animal roared and charged towards the nets, they dropped it and ran. Ignoring them, the tiger had bolted into the nearest patch of thick undergrowth. It seemed to be a tiger who didn't want to mess with people, Rohan thought. "Most tigers prefer to leave people alone," Carpet Sahib confirmed. "I always believe that the tiger is the gentleman among the big cats but the trouble is people won't leave tigers alone."

He had been sitting under a tree watching what was happening from a distance – when the tiger flashed out, he brought it to the cave. It would have been better if the forest department had managed to net the tiger, he said. Then it could have been released in another territory far away from the village clusters. Now the tiger would have to be guided safely through, avoiding railway tracks and highways without leaving pugmarks.

It was better that no one knew where the tiger had gone. "People have forgotten how to live with tigers now. It becomes a disruption in their lives." For Carpet Sahib who never actually spoke aloud, that was a long conversation – Rohan had never heard him so worried before. He seemed to sigh. "The other point is that someone else saw me."

"Saw you?" Rohan started. He knew that he and Manjul could see Carpet Sahib, bhoot or otherwise and so could animals, but no one else had seen him before – not even that year when the leopard was guided by Carpet Sahib and Manjul into the school laboratory through crowds of nosy people munching food and eager to see whether anyone would get eaten or the leopard would be shot. For them, it was always more *tamasha* than anything else.

Carpet Sahib had been leading the tiger through a dip in the forest when they passed a gnarled old banyan tree. It was a grey shape in the early morning haze, almost like an elephant with squirrels running up and down the trunk and a monkey swinging in the branches. "I knew there was someone there, I could sense him." It was an old sadhu tucked away between the wooden pillars that the banyan had sent out – he was almost the same colour as the wood with tangled hair, very easy to miss if you hadn't known that he was there. He was smoking a chillum and the blue vapour was losing itself in coiled trails in the sunlight. "*Hoom, firang,*" a hoarse voice croaked suddenly. "You're a long way from the Kumaon trails."

"What's more, he recognized me." There was a note of surprise in Carpet Sahib's voice.

"Um, was he also..." Rohan asked, stumbling over the 'g' word that came to his lips.

Carpet Sahib's face broke into a smile. "He could have been, but he felt real. For a moment I thought it was the sadhu they talk about, the one who has an ashram and kept a tiger as his pet 80 years ago. But I could feel him – he was human." Carpet Sahib and the tiger sat under the banyan tree talking to the sadhu. The tiger was sniffing and snuffling, its ears pricked up. At one point he bounded up, dashed into the bushes and they heard squealing and thrashing. "He's killed a pig," observed the sadhu. And a little while later, the tiger came back dragging a pig's carcass and began crunching bones and tearing flesh. It ignored the sadhu completely. "That could have meant he was a bhoot!" Carpet Sahib laughed. "But I think he smelt of trees and smoke and dirt. Nothing human. The tiger couldn't smell him — that's why many sadhus live happily in tiger country. Unless it's a tiger like the Champawat maneater that doesn't care what the smell is as long as it can be eaten."

Rohan thought of a sadhu he had met in the Sunderbans who slept in tiger country where no one else, not even the honey collectors, dared to tread. "Was it only the smell? How did you understand him?" he asked.

"I read his mind, like I read yours. Thoughts don't have a language. He told me that there is a tribal hunt that the villagers carry out every year. Normally they only kill squirrels or a few deer. This year they have big game in mind. They think their forest god sent them the tiger. However, he couldn't tell me when it was."

As they talked, the shadows lengthened. "We shall have to start moving soon," Carpet Sahib said. He rose out of the grass. The elephant rumbled softly and as Rohan got up; it reached out and picked him up again. Rohan was getting quite used to this riding an elephant bareback thing. He settled and waited. Though he was looking at the mouth of the cave, he almost missed it. The tiger slunk out so well camouflaged by the stripes of evening sunlight and shadow that it almost seemed like a rippling patch of forest floor. It was pebbly and rocky terrain, though the path that had been made by feet was still there. The sadhu had said that the cave was a holy place because Baba Ram Swarup had housed his pet tiger there all those years ago but pilgrims had stopped visiting it. A look into the ashram was enough for them. Some of the older villagers still remembered where the cave was, but they were too old and toothless to make the effort themselves. Nor was there anything of value in the cave like beehives and honey that would have interested the younger people, so it remained empty and bat ridden except for a few trekkers who went through the forest, took photographs of the rock outcrops and went away again.

Now, as darkness fell, there was even less chance of meeting anyone. Birds settled in the trees, a firefly began to flash somewhere and others joined in. In between the flashes it was utterly dark. Rohan's phone began to ring. It was his mother wanting to know where he was. "The uncles haven't called – have you met them yet?"

"No Ma," he told her. "I haven't got back. I'll talk to them, I promise." He could feel the man laughing and wondered whether that was telepathy as well. But then the phone rang again and this time it was the Khan Sahib on the other end.

"I hope you're not in the forest."

"Why, Khan Uncle?"

"We have word that the villagers are taking out a hunting party tonight. The forest department here lacks the manpower to tackle the situation. Get back as fast as you can."

abu had worried and worried at the situation. He could try going to the Pradhan, but then pradhans didn't listen to children, so he did the next best thing, which was tell Master Moshai. Someone with Maoist friends was bound to have a solution, he thought. He caught him after class when Master Moshai already had one leg over the back of his bicycle. "What is it Habu?" Master Moshai sounded a little irritated. "Didn't you understand today's story?" He was late for his tuition and didn't like the idea of pedalling furiously to get there.

Habu told him what he had overheard. Master Moshai put his leg back on the ground. "Are you sure? Tell me all over again." Habu dutifully repeated everything, not sure why he was doing it in the first place. "And who was the man?"

"Bangeshwari Murmu." He thought the Master Moshai would go promptly to the Pradhan and tell him what had happened but instead the Master Moshai stood there and thought about it. "Did he say when the hunt would be?" he asked. Habu shook his head. "Then we have to find out. After that we can tell the Pradhan."

Finding out entailed a lot of tiptoeing through the narrow alleys behind the lines of huts while women like Habu's mother were busy cooking and cleaning in their homes and walking into a few deserted barns where there were bundles of dried straw waiting to be carried out to the cattle sheds. It was surprising how light-footed the lanky Master Moshai could be. He riffled through the straw and looked around the bundles. "Whatever was here is gone," he said.

"How do you know there was anything there at all?" Habu asked in fascination. Master Moshai picked up a stick and showed Habu the tapered end. "The head fits here. This was thrown away because it was badly shaped."

From the barn, they crossed to the open fields. The pundit was walking through the long grass swinging a brass pot in one hand – his puja pot, not the morning-in-the-fields one. "Arré Pundit Moshai, whom did you bless?" Master Moshai called out. The pundit checked, saw Habu and the teacher and smiled a greeting as he said cheerfully, "Oh, the shikar party – they asked me to bless them before they started out."

Habu wondered a little at that but kept his eyes respectfully down – the pundit had a habit of complaining to parents. Master Moshai nodded and waved and they stood and watched him pass. "This one wants to show me a plant he found," Master Moshai jerked his thumb at Habu which Habu thought was quite unnecessary. "Let's go," and he steered Habu in the opposite direction from where the pundit had come. The moment they were under cover of the trees, Habu doubled back to the clump of trees from which the pundit had emerged. He knew it well because of the big old mango tree that he and the others pelted green mangoes down from in spring and climbed in summer. Who owned the tree no one knew. It had been there for ages. Master Moshai caught up with him and put a hand on his shoulder to slow him down. "The shikar party is it... Mind the bushes."

To their right a deer bounded away in a sharp rustle of undergrowth. A bird called. "It's seen something…" Master Moshai said. And there was a twanging sound, followed by a sharp *thak*. Whatever it was had missed the deer and hit the tree branch where the bird was sitting, making it flutter into the air in a beat of wings and feathers.

"Arré you call that good aim? How are you going to hit a tiger like that?" a loud voice guffawed before being shushed by a series of hisses.

"They're not even careful," said Master Moshai and he edged his way towards the voices, gesturing to Habu to stay put. Habu saw him disappear rapidly and stood there deciding whether to climb up the tree and see what was going on or just stay there and keep an eye out for the pundit in case he came back. It was a nice way to spend the afternoon, better than sitting with his exercise books and practising sums or handwriting.

While Habu was waiting, he thought he saw a snake slithering through the shadows and was thinking seriously of climbing a tree – to his relief Master Moshai returned. He had his phone in his hand. "You took pictures of them?" "Habu asked eagerly. "Let me see!"

"My camera phone is noisy, so I recorded them instead of taking pictures. Now let's go and talk to the Pradhan!"

When the Pradhan heard the recording, he put his head in his hands. "This after the visit from the forest department! Do you know where they are going?"

"They were meeting some others from Alija and Salboni. One of them is an expert tracker. What should we do?"

"You send a WhatsApp of the recording to your friends. However, an official letter also has to be written to the head forest babu in Kolkata. The babus do nothing unless they have three copies in writing." The Pradhan pulled out the drawer of his desk and brought out pen and paper. "I will write

Master Moshai and you can correct my English, if I make any mistakes."

Master Moshai was busy with the green and white dots in his phone. So Habu asked, "What will you write?" peering rudely and curiously over the Pradhan's shoulder. The Pradhan's pen scratched away and Habu found most of it too complicated. Very often he scratched out words. The Master Moshai came to join Habu at the desk and was promptly drawn into composing the letter. Between him and the Pradhan it seemed to take forever and when they were finally satisfied, it had to be copied out in fair on another sheet of paper with the Pradhan's name and address on it.

To,

Principle Chief Conservator of Forests (Wildlife)
and Chief Wildlife Warden, West Bengal
Bikash Bhawan,
Sector 2, Salt Lake City,
Kolkata – 700091

Subject: Appeal to prevent mass slaughter of wildlife by armed hunters in Southern West Bengal

Sir,

As you are well aware, members of tribal communities in South-western West Bengal engage in very large-scale hunting of all forms of wildlife across the year. Such hunts take place on the occasion of various tribal festivals as well as on randomly chosen dates in absence of any festival. Thousands of hunters congregate in various forest and non-forest areas and kill or capture any wild animal that they find. Tens of thousands of mammals, birds and reptiles die every day during these mass hunts, causing irreparable damage to biodiversity. This may cause local extinction of many species of endangered fauna. Many of these species are protected under Schedule I and II of Wildlife Protection Act, 1972. These include Monitor Lizards, Jungle Cat, Fishing Cat, Indian Palm Civet, Indian Grey Mongoose, Golden Jackal, Indian Wolf, Common Rat Snake and numerous species of birds. It is of prime worry that these hunters may poach a Royal Bengal Tiger in Baghghora near Lalgarh.

We will provide you with all information and assistance that you may need to stop this event.

Sincerely,

Mohan Pradhan

"The letter has to be posted," the Pradhan said. "Unless it reaches the forest babus, they will never believe it. Take it to Binpur for me." He held it out to Master Moshai.

"I was going to Binpur anyway," Master Moshai said putting the letter into his kurta pocket. "I teach the Constable's son. Habu go home now, there's school tomorrow." Habu followed him back to his bicycle, watched him mount it and heard the bicycle bell ringing as he went down the track and out of sight. He wondered where would the tiger he had never seen, except for its paw print, be now.

14

aghghora, a bare plateau on the top of a hillock surrounded by jungles on either side; there Bondebota had once led a tiger round and round in rings until the beast had collapsed from exhaustion. Today yellow sandstone and black rock marked that legendary tiger's stripes. Baghghora was sacred to the tribals of 12 villages – every five years they gathered there to make their contract with the Lord of the Jungle. And every hunting party that set out ended up there to light a bonfire. The sadhu was delighted to tell Carpet Sahib that story after they had flushed him out again.

It was not Corbett territory – that is why Carpet Sahib seemed a little at a loss. But then did bhoots get lost? Rohan thought he should ask

Manjul about that – she seemed to be an authority on anything ghostly. Now, however, they were faced with a tiger hunt and they had no idea which way to go. He didn't like the way the sadhu hidden in the banyan was chuckling either – the thought of getting the better of a *firang* seemed the best joke he had heard in a long while. Having determined the direction of Baghghora – and it was the way from which the wind was blowing – they took a sharp turn towards the slope of the nearest hill. The tiger ran in front, occasionally startling pigs from the undergrowth and checking back as if it were consulting them. The elephant, however, moved on smoothly, never faltering. It seemed to have a direction in mind.

The closest they came to people was a hut on the edge of a grove of trees with a fence of stakes around it. The tiger went over to the stakes and sniffed; then Rohan saw the glowing eyes turn up in their direction before the tiger moved on again. They startled some night crows and a deer as the road they were on became a path, then became a track and climbed steeply. The trees thinned and they were out on a plateau that the had to cross – Rohan was aware that he and the animals were exposed and if anyone happened to be watching, they could be in danger. But both the animals and Carpet Sahib were untroubled. They crossed the plateau and as they reached the trees fringing the other side, the elephant threw up its head and its ears flapped. Then it raised its trunk and trumpeted. Immediately there was a host of answering trumpets from the trees and a crashing and crunching. "Its herd is here," Carpet Sahib announced. "They come from the range of hills that form the boundary." Another elephant came out of the shadows and raised its trunk at them as if in greeting. Rohan's elephant went forward and the two snuffed at each other. Rohan realized that the shadows behind the second elephant were moving but whatever was in those shadows did not come forward. Instead, the tiger moved out of the open ground into the shadows behind the elephant and the new elephant did not baulk or raise its feet threateningly.

Then the second elephant turned and went back into the shadows. The tiger did not reappear. "Where's it gone?" Rohan wanted to know.

"The elephants will take it across the border," Carpet Sahib answered as the elephant under them began turning back. A tiger escorted by a herd of elephants would have been something to see. Rohan wondered whether the herd would lose its nerve half way and turn on the tiger. "Think about it," Carpet Sahib told him, reading his thoughts. "Elephants destroy camera traps — they hate them. And they help tigers go unseen. Actually, though they may be enemies, they are there to defend their homes from people. Hunters kill both elephants and tigers depending on what gets them the most money. Don't worry — the tiger will be safe for now and go back to where he came from."

All at once, Rohan yawned widely and lay down on the elephant's neck — it was probably because all the tension he had been through was suddenly off his shoulders. The neck smelt of strong musky elephant sweat, but he was too tired to mind that. It was broad enough for him to rest his head on and it moved like a rocking chair under him. Sway, yawn, rock, his eyes gradually closed. He thought Carpet Sahib was there behind him, but he wasn't sure.

The ride seemed to go on and on — he thought he saw a tiger walking in step with the elephant and the rocks were moving around them, dark silhouettes surrounding him and the tiger. They went in and out of darkness and Rohan couldn't tell how much time had passed — he was too sleepy to raise his wrist and look at his watch. He was far too comfortable, hard elephant back and all. Then all at once he heard a sharp metallic clanging and a shout of, "Orre baba! Haathi! Do something…no, what's that, a boy on the elephant's back…"

And then he was carefully deposited on a patch of hard ground. "Madam, he just got back! His elephant brought him!"

"That's ridiculous," Rohan thought, his last thought before he went back to sleep.

15

The uncles firmly removed Rohan from the bungalow the next morning. "We can't have you disappearing again when you have to go back home very soon," Khan Sahib told him. The Rajbari, of course, was very grand, though a little moth-eaten around the edges with frayed curtains and carpets. He sat on the long verandah with a plate heaped with *luchi* and *torkari* in front of him, while the Major and the Khan Sahib put him through a series of cross-examinations. His mother was not talking to him. "I'm going to call his father," she announced, "and say that he's getting out of hand. No targets set, no homework! If you can get some sense into him, Khan Sahib, please do."

"This is the time," the Major said, "when you have to figure out what you want to do with your life. If you have a good plan, your parents will accept it."

"I haven't thought," Rohan answered through a mouthful of luchi torkari.

"Manjul wants to join the forest department," the Khan Sahib pointed out. "Is that something you would like to do?" Getting grilled first thing in the morning after everything that had happened the day before was annoying; however, that was the way adults were.

"How could you possibly run away on a wild elephant?" the Major exploded. Rohan looked at a flattened luchi silently. There was no answer he could give which would make any sense — encounters with tigers were never questioned, or even that leopard they led into the laboratory, but being kidnapped by a wild elephant?

"What did you say?" Manjul asked when he called her.

"They said you were more disciplined than I was!"

"*Baapre*! And then?"

"It's actually because Ma was on their case," Rohan said. "There's no other reason. I told them that I wanted to go into conservation and after a while they stopped pestering me."

Also the Forest officials had dropped in, a man and a woman. They were accompanied by a lanky non-official looking young man who they said was the Dharia schoolmaster. After the formal greetings and their amazement at Rohan's exploits on elephant back, they announced that they had asked for volunteers to help track the tiger and Master Moshai was helping them. The uncles had almost exploded all over again at that. "We're very short staffed here," Joydip explained. "It isn't a tiger reserve, so sixty per cent of the posts are vacant."

"And two of your people gassed themselves," the Major observed, rather nastily.

The Khan Sahib intervened hastily, "I'm sure that's a good idea, but if the volunteers don't have some experience, it may do more harm than good." "Well Master Moshai thinks it may work," Joydip said. "He's very familiar with the forests. He's the one who first WhatsApped the pugmark to us."

Purabi added, "And he's warned us about the hunting parties. He brought an official letter from the Pradhan too."

They were full of plans – the drones had not found anything useful, so perhaps they could get some sniffer dogs to find the tiger? And with every idea they kept looking hopefully at the Major and the Khan Sahib. "What will you do when you find the tiger?" the Khan Sahib wanted to know. "I mean, manage to catch it."

"Shift it to some other territory – it doesn't belong here in any case."

"Weren't you talking about a hulla party?" the Major wanted to know.

"Oh yes," Joydip and Purabi said together – then Purabi stopped and let Joydip continue. "That was to take care of the elephant problem."

There was always money for hulla parties in the Midnapore area because elephant raids were only too common. The parties were made up of groups of local boys armed with a long wooden stick with a jute bag tied to one end. To Rohan's horror, the jute bag had a sharp metal spear head sticking out of it. The bag was dipped in petrol or any engine oil and set on fire before the party went chasing elephants out of a village. Rohan told Manjul that the Forest officials were planning to go to Baghghora because that was mentioned in the letter. The whole thing was apparently the Master Moshai's idea. "Go chasing elephants and you may be able to chase the tiger away too and scare the hunters."

They took a truck load of hulla people, odds and ends, Rohan thought. Some were excited at the thought of tracking elephants, a boy called Habu who declared that he had found the first paw print and who stayed close to the Master Moshai. They bumped their way up to Laljola and then towards Baghghora – not that Rohan recognized any of it because the elephants had steered clear of the roads, barring a few mad dashes across a highway. It was like a picnic in a way – people handed around singaras and cups of tea. There was a discussion as to whether they should stop at a dhaba for dinner after it was all over.

"If I fail in school, I can always join a hulla party," Rohan told Manjul – "there's always money to pay for chasing elephants out of paddy fields."

Manjul snorted on the other end of the line. "No wonder the uncles said I was more disciplined than you were. Did you see *him* again?"

"No," Rohan answered sadly. "Though I met the sadhu again and he asked me where the firang had gone. Luckily the uncles thought he was stoned."

The sadhu was sitting where they had left him the night before. He startled the whole party with his booming "Hoom!" and even Rohan, who should have expected it. After confusing everyone by asking about the Englishman, he said there had been an elephant, perhaps even a tiger…his eyes flickered once in Rohan's direction…and yes, there had some people doing some kind of *tamasha* who had stopped to share a *chillum* with him. They had gone towards Baghghora, he added gesturing before subsiding into the gnarled roots around him.

Walking was not so much fun, since they were all asked to be as quiet as possible until they reached the plateau. The way was pebbly and people slid and tripped, occasionally being pricked by thorns and cursing, "*Eh sala*! Elephants here? Not possible."

The shouts and the blazing bags startled the hunters. The cow obviously knew it was in no danger – it was munching leaves when the party burst out of the bushes with its flaming bags.

An arrow went off and hit a tree, luckily not one of the group. "What are you doing here with that cow?" Joydip demanded. The hunters looked at each other. "It's that annual hunt," one of them muttered.

"Yes, but what are you hunting with that cow?"

"They've come to hunt tigers," one of the hulla party shouted out. The two men looked very guilty when they heard that and started to babble something. In the meanwhile, the Major and the Khan Sahib went around the area with their torches. "A tiger has been here," the Major said running the beam up and down, "but its tracks are almost wiped out by those of the elephants." Joydip went to see and agreed with him.

"You do know," Joydip said to the hunters, "That killing a tiger means jail?" He flashed his torch on their faces as he spoke. The light caught the glint of their eyes. "We haven't killed anything yet," one of them mumbled.

"Lucky for you," said the Master Moshai. "You'd better come back with us on the truck. Go hunting with the rest during the day tomorrow." The cow was pushed onto the truck as well, which caused more good-humoured laughter, though the two hunters huddled in one corner and glared.

They weren't any happier when they were put into the Binpur lock up for the night as a warning. "What happened to the cow?" Manjul wanted to know.

"That kid Habu adopted it," Rohan said. "He apparently takes the cows grazing before school like you do."

"Hopefully his father won't mind another cow to feed!" Manjul retorted.

"I hadn't thought of that!" Rohan said.

Of course, he hadn't thought of a lot of things. His mother insisted that he apologise to Bablu Mama for misusing his hospitality. Then there was the caretaker's old cycle he had abandoned by the side of the road when the elephant ran off with him – he had managed to leave word with the Master Moshai about that but decided against mentioning it to either the uncles or his mother. It might mean calculating pocket money to buy another cycle if it wasn't found.

he tiger would be safe with the elephants unless they tried to cross a railway line or a highway. The railways had been slower in his time, the man who had been Jim Corbett thought as he sat on a hillock. Life was getting more and more complicated – before he had walked through the Kumaon forests at night without encountering a soul – just the deer and the pig and a solitary tigress that would growl a warning, provided it wasn't a maneater. Now people were jostling for space with trees and animals and because it was a people's world, animals were losing.

He had seen leopards beaten to death because the big cats had invaded homes and schools looking for a cosy hiding place. Now, whenever he could, he guided leopards and tigers away from people.

He could follow them at night by the trails they left like paths of light in the darkness.

This tiger had been rescued at the right time – the elephants would guide him back to their hills and he hoped from there it would go to Neora or even Nepal – the man had seen tribal hunts as well as the Maharajah's hunts, hordes of people chasing one single animal while the woodlands were disturbed with crashes and clangs. He had hunted for the Maharajahs himself at one time – it had meant good money being in the forests he loved. Then he had gone on to hunt the maneaters, finally realising that it was best to make sure that people and animals didn't bump into each other and capture big cats on camera.

After a while, people would stop looking for the tiger and the villagers would settle down to daily lives and forget that they had ever seen a pugmark. Grandmothers would tell the children stories about it at night when they put them to sleep. In the end, it would just be a story and nothing more.

He watched the light in the distance fade and sighed. It was time to return to the hills where he belonged. There was an old wooden chair waiting for him on the verandah – a chair that he missed when he was away in the jungle for long periods.

At Kaladhungi, one of the guards suddenly saw a blue flicker of light from the house – it didn't look like a firefly. He quickly began walking towards where he'd seen it and almost collided with the other guard who shared his watch. "Seen a ghost?" the second guard asked.

He told him about the blue light. "There it is again!" he cried pointing as he saw the flash again. The other guard didn't even bother to turn. "Leave it, *yaar*. It's only Carpet Sahib."

Rahul's Afterword

Think about a world with no fire. Think about a world where we waited very, very long for our food.

Well, once upon a time, not very long ago, when dogs weren't pets and fire was out of our grasp, we were afraid to wander the woods at night. The only sources of light in the deep, dark forests were from the moon on a cloudless night, a dark sky full of stars, and some pretty fireflies cruising among long lush grasses. Amidst this scattered glitter, through the thickly bunched leaves, two pairs of yellow-green eyes pierced through the night. These eyes were unchallenged. No one dared look at them.

For many, many years, the big cats have been on the top of the food chain. The tigers would kill the deer. Eat the best parts. Then the jackals and hyenas would come and pick their leftovers. We made do with whatever little was left. The deer was too fast for us to catch. The tiger too strong to challenge.

Then one day, two stones clicked together and some sparks flew. Just by chance, fire was discovered.

This accident upset years and years of evolution. The big cats were confused. What was this red flame that was so hot that it hurt them? They were not used to being challenged. Ever. This accident swooshed us to the top of the food chain, jumping over the hyenas, lions, tigers and all the powerful animals you can think of. We suddenly felt stronger.

Today big cages are built around these powerful animals and they are kept in what we call a zoo. If you entered that cage, with no weapon, do you think you could beat the beast?

Discovering fire was an accident and this upset Mother Nature. Overnight, the food chain was disrupted. If you suddenly grew up one day, bigger and stronger than the biggest kid in your school, would you bully the kid? Be mean to the person?

Why do we bully these big cats? Is it because we think we are stronger? What if, just like we found fire, they find a way to beat us?

But that's not possible you think! Well, once upon a time, not very long ago, that's what they thought.

Acknowledgements

For Vijay who believes in Carpet Sahib and the magic of tigers.

Aditi for her poem.

Nainital and corbett for being the sources of inspiration that they are – not to mention the ghost tiger that crossed the road.

The team at TERI for their support and belief in the books.